FROM AUNTY AYESHA AND THE JINNS WITH LOVE

DECODING DESI MARRIAGES

(^ comes with traditional values and modern solutions)

For the about to be wed, the newlyweds and especially for those who've been wed for decades.

AF451248

Published by Liberty Publishing
C-16, Sector 31-A, Mehran Town Extension,
Korangi Industrial Area, Karachi, Pakistan

1 2 3 4 5 6 7 8 9 10

ISBN 978_627_7626_35_8

Printed and bound in Pakistan

It's not the same road. There's never a one-size-fits-all. The dawns vary as do the dusks. The afternoons are always uncertain, and come what may is just what amas tell their betis to ease their hearts. Nevertheless, all men share a common trait: the ability to melt like a Rs. 10 Walls ice-lolly. May this guide be your key to defrosting your man and your life.

Dedication

For **Malik Muzaffar Saeed,** my dear baba - a man who, despite all odds, managed to be the best husband he could be, the father many would want, and whose boundless love for his wife, children, and all around him, I have seen in no other man.

For **Farhan Suleman,** my dear husband - the one who makes life a lot less chaotic, the gentle balm for my restless heart, and the embodiment of the Autumn wind in human form.

For **Forty - Feel Good Gummies,** which helped me catch up on some much-needed deep sleep to travel to realms unknown to mankind.

And **FroGurt,** the new frozen yogurt pop-up in the city, whose 360 grams of Pina Colada yogurt goodness was my daily companion in writing this book.

Table of Contents

XXX

Chapter 1

Choosing Chaudhry

My nano once said men are like sweaters in a wholesale shop. You'll always find one that's too big, one that's too small, one that you'll fit into if you stop stuffing *ghee chapatis* but...the perfect fit is a rare and treasured event. And so, choosing a man is no different than choosing a sweater. But before choosing a man, let us choose a sweater. And remember, my dear friend, a good sweater can change lives.

When you enter the shop, you very well know your size; you're a medium. You've always been a medium. You can juggle between a medium and a medium-large, but you will never ask for a 3XL or an XS right? Because, no way will those ever be good fits, despite how well-knit and beautifully coloured. Similarly, in man-terms, deep down you *know* that some things just won't work out and are deal breakers and cannot be compromised on, so no matter how appealing the man is or how many green flags he's holding, if he's not your size, don't grab him off the shelf. Droopy sleeves fall in gravies and get stains that don't come off and elbow-length sleeves make one shiver on cold, smoggy nights.

A Peshawari man I once knew was attracted to his workaholic cousin, and on most occasions he had told her how his type is a woman who is fully dependent on her spouse for emotional and financial needs. The two fell in love and out of sheer love he said that he'd make an exception for her. Did he? Of course, he was a man of his word. He let her work and make her decisions, but, in doing so, he became aggressive, less-thoughtful, and borderline abusive.

Now, not all Peshawari men are like that. But men in general, when in love, become children. They start to build dreams with the same tenderness with which their *amis* knitted winter shawls, dreams that are colourful, vibrant, and often too large for their own good. But once that dream becomes repetitive, and the rainbow-like-colours become blinding, men forget how to act. Much like sweaters, if I may. You can only stretch a sweater too much, before it either rips apart or bounces back to its size - the size the cousin forcefully wore.

Then, as life would have it, there was a friend of a friend whose husband would snap at the thought of his wife pursuing her passion for coding in a male-dominated office, *assuming* that she'd run away with one of the coder colleagues. To him, the main issue was that he could not comprehend how coding worked, and hence - thinking about his wife writing *encrypted messages to her potential suitors* was a thought that many wise men his age could have. That friend of a friend was completely smitten with that anti-coder man, and so she gave up her career that she greatly felt for, only to realize that her husband's suspicion would also arise when it'd take a minute or more to pick up her Johnny & Jugnu order from the gate. And then, she'd spend hours explaining to him what had happened, until the wrap would get sad and soggy and a baby corn would drop out of sheer embarrassment for that friend of a friend. That man was not a good fit for her, in fact, he was not a good fit for anyone. He was a poorly manufactured sweater that ought to have been discarded long ago. But oftentimes, the oldest, most worn out sweaters are displayed on the front rows.

There are also times when you get a sweater that has all the qualities that you've ever wanted in life. It fits. It's your colour. It buttons up but lets you breathe. It makes you feel *you*. But then, one day, on a cold night when you definitely need it, you just don't feel like wearing it anymore. You would rather shiver. It's not that it doesn't fit like before - it almost still does and that faded colour is beautiful too, but the threads that occasionally tickle have started to sting.

This is the story of the *ama jee* of a dear friend who I no longer talk to for some reason I do not recall. Her *ama* married a handsome young gentleman from the army. It was one of those arranged marriages where both the families loved each other, and the couple's love only grew over the initial years. They had two children; my friend and her brother. After my friend got married, her parents started to drift apart. Her *ama jaan* and *abu jee* realized that though the attachment to each other remained - *aadat*, as they termed it - they had wanted to part ways for a long time but something ongoing in life had prevented them from doing so. They were both very good people, but not entirely good for each other and it took them time to comprehend that. There was always the option to not let go, for an eternity had been spent, but both of them were excited to do the exact opposite. There were no tears and grievances - just *logoun ki baatein*. Sometimes, you outgrow a well-worn sweater. And then someone else gets to wear the sweater you once proudly owned. And that's life.

There are also times when a button gets loose, or there's no button to begin with, or the colour is not the colour you've always wanted, or that the sweater is manufactured in Sialkot; a place you've never desired to visit. But, these are minor hindrances and a spoonful of compromise can make the imperfections worth the while. Let's take the example of my studious and successful auntie Feroza, who dreamed of marrying a man with achievements akin to hers. Yet she found herself wedded to her second cousin, who was a BA dropout, and knew nothing about the events of the world, other than the daily happenings of Chorangi, and called his mustache *chota sher*. He was far from what she had envisioned and to her it seemed like their marriage would collapse after the very first day, for the differences between them seemed insurmountable and their worlds poles apart. She had received the sweater as a gift which she had no choice but to accept, and *to her*, the sweater was not her size, her colour, her fabric, or her fit. But the gift giver here was a rather learned person, who saw beneath the surface and the only thing he instructed Feroza to do, was to give it time. The only compromise she had to make was to hold on to the sweater - to give it a chance, to hang it in her wardrobe. And let me tell you, she's holding onto the sweater to this very day and she wouldn't have it any other way.

There are women, who I refer to as summer ladies. Even as the colder months descend and their husband-less rooms grow chillier than some frostbitten hearts, these women find no need for a sweater. Some pretend that they're warm enough whilst others are well-equipped to face the challenges of life that the longing of a soul sleeping next to them is not something they're willing to incorporate. These women aren't opposed to the idea of sweaters—they just don't feel the need to seek one out. Some of them live vibrant, fulfilled lives, while others might harbor a few regrets. Over time, a number of these summer ladies find themselves warming up to the colder seasons, and when they *do* decide to go sweater shopping, the choices are slimmer, but the old rules of finding the right fit still apply.

Back in the summer of 2015, I weighed in at a hefty 78 kg. I was 20 kg over my usual weight and I would often go to the nearby park to walk. I hardly saw corpulent people like me there, but rather fit ones with their t-shirts matching their water bottles and sneakers. They seemed like they had it all figured out. There I was, jogging awkwardly in my old, but trusty Crocs, struggling to juggle my water bottle and phone. In a bid to blend in, I splurged on some matching Pumas that looked great with my t-shirt. It felt nice, sort of a boost from the inside, but those Pumas were a disaster—pinching my pinky toe, chafing my ankles, and before long, I was relegated to the "old-aunty bench" barely twenty minutes into my walk.

An aunty, who appeared to be my nano's age, and was in much better shape than me, put down the book in her hand and shifted her glance to me. I smiled at her. For the next forty minutes or so, we talked. We chatted about our respective house help, the polluted sky being the aftermath of an American conspiracy, and most importantly, we talked about men. She told me that she had been married twice, and had married three of her daughters off, and so there was nothing about men that she did not know.

She confided that her first marriage was born out of love, a rarity along with being somewhat scandalous at that time and so the obstacles that came with accepting her were inevitable. And it was only a decade but thankfully no child later, when she came to realize that in Pakistani society, you do not *wed a man, you wed the entire family.* She mused that there's not much harm in that, unless the family consisted of a bunch of privacy-invading lunatics, which hers didn't. The problem lay in her *cowardless* husband, who could not keep a bedroom secret and anything that she did, and each step she took, became the talk of the town. Over time, her obsession with their mansion and the pink satin bed sheets from London that got dry cleaned each week in that very mansion, wore off and she finally came to a conclusion that she had in fact, married a one-size-fits-all sweater. In men-terms, sweaters aren't meant to be shared. They can be passed on, but not shared.

Her second and current husband did not come from money and could not make money, but he brought her an immense sense of peace and comfort—exactly what she had been searching for. It took her nearly a whole TV season to figure it out, but she realized she had found a sweater made from local, humble materials, yet it promised never to tear and fit almost as if it was made-to-order. And on the off chance it did tear, a quick run through with the sewing machine was all it took to make it as good as new.

The most striking realization she shared was that not all women can intuitively pick a sweater that suits them perfectly, and her eldest daughter was a textbook example. The daughter expected a lot, which is not wrong, for a woman must know her value, but she was persistent on finding someone well-established, handsome, tall, and utterly compatible, leading her to dismiss many suitable suitors. Aunty made her realize that though she had a well reputed job, she wished to not work after marriage, which was fine, and since she had always been job oriented, she didn't like to cook and basic chores to her were tedious. But what if her ideal man enjoyed a delicious homemade *mutton handi* on weekends, a dish she was reluctant to even attempt? What if he preferred a healthier lifestyle and did not believe in women being out of shape? Because aunty's eldest was as she termed it, an adrak; sprouting unpredictably in all directions.

Eventually, the eldest came to terms with the reality and settled with a short and loving man who wasn't the wealthiest, but he made sure that all that his wife wanted, his wife got. As he approached thirty, he began losing quite a bit of his hair, but his wife found no room for complaint. To her, he was, and still is, the most wonderful husband and father.

The second daughter, a homebody who loved gardening and brewed the perfect *karak* chai, agreed to go along with her parents' wishes when it came to marriage. Aunty admitted that in this instance, she was at fault for overlooking the importance of compatibility, assuming her daughter would adapt as she always had. While her daughter did manage to adjust, she didn't find joy in the marriage. The sweater fit but felt uncomfortable and restrictive on tougher days, sometimes proving too burdensome to wear. Early into their marriage, challenges necessitated a sit-down discussion between both families. It took time, but gradually, the couple found their rhythm. The husband came to understand that marriage is a two-way street and recognized the need to adjust his behavior. Not all men come to such a realization—sometimes it's spurred by an epiphany, other times it's driven by familial pressure. In their case, it was definitely the latter. Now, they're a happy couple, different in many ways but aligned in what matters. Aunty mentioned that they haven't been on a vacation in a while because they can't agree on a destination. But, as she chuckled, that's the kind of problem they don't mind having.

Aunty's third daughter, considered the most beautiful of the sisters by societal standards, developed a speech issue following an illness in her teenage years. Despite numerous sessions with various speech therapists, her condition only deteriorated over time. Aunty feared that despite her luscious long curls and maiden-like fair skin, she would not find a suitable suitor at all. Indeed, when the daughter reached thirty-six, she resigned herself to the possibility that a soulmate wasn't in her destiny. As life would have it, the family's then neighbour, a divorced lad whose wife was electrocuted and had passed shortly after, showed interest in making aunty's third born his wife. He was a year younger, and had a daughter and two pet cats - if we're counting all household members. Aunty recalled that she couldn't help but remember the cats because of how fondly he spoke of them. During their first formal meeting over tea, he mentioned his feline companions several times. Her third daughter who had grown stubborn over the years due to the never ending *rishta* process, happily accepted the neighbour with his daughter *and the cats*. Aunty remarked that among all her daughters, the third one turned out to be the happiest. Her husband not only supported her but also encouraged her lifelong dream by helping her open her own salon. It seemed her perfect sweater had been just next door all along, and only when the time was right did she get to wear it. The joy it brought was immense, a clear testament to the timing of fate.

———

Dear Ayesha,

Men are not sweaters. They are fairly complex beings. Some have minds that govern, hearts that are loving and souls that are resilient and they, like the brave men of ancient times, find solace in their partner's embrace. Others are, well, less redeemable and quite frankly sometimes, rotten and ought to be whisked away by a sinister wind for their misdeeds. The latter are not ideal for companionship and should be left alone to wander the world until they better themselves. The wise say that it is the job of a woman to love and forgive the wandering man, but that woman is not his partner, but his mother.

And yes, females, though fascinating creatures, should not have to spend a lifetime unraveling the complexities of men, for what a waste of time that would be, so for now we can settle with men being knitted balls of wool - easier to grasp, but still with a few tangles.

Love, the jinns.

Chapter 2

Fixing Faisal

When a man spends twenty or so years a certain way, his ways cannot completely change after marriage. Good sex, a scrumptious tiffin and a few praises may make him keep the towel in its place but it will not entirely make him a new man. Just as a woman hopes to be embraced for who she is—often tweaking her habits to better mesh with her partner's life—a man may not always return the favor with the same zeal. Now, not all men are like that, but even the finest kind, take time in changing their ways if need be.

Back in 1880, my *ama's* cousin who we called *khala* (until she moved to the UK and urged us to call her by her name Angelica and not Aaabida), got a food processor set at the time of her marriage to a Faislabad tycoon. It was not that her husband could not afford one himself, but a *"sensible"* woman's father did not let her go to her new house without all the equipment she would ever need and not need, even a wiper; to wipe the wet floors, of course, not her tears. When the food processor was unpacked and set to use, it was discovered that it seemingly did not work. No one bothered to read through the manual, until years after, when the probable cause of it not working was that of voltage inconsistencies. Later, the machine worked when plugged in at the outside kitchen but faltered in the inside kitchen. However, former khala Aabida, due to the scorching heat, and her own stubborn pride of having to use the machine in the servant kitchen would always plug it inside, despite knowing the problem. This caused the food to not be shredded properly and eventually the very expensive and hardly-used machine gave up and stopped working entirely. Had she understood the machine's needs - the fact that the voltage issue was external and not in her or the machine's control, that partially shredded *sabzi* gets stuck between teeth and are a nuisance to eat, and that her ego was not worth sacrificing a well-built machine that usually lasts a lifetime, things would have turned out quite differently.

I understand that she blamed the machine, for her friends had gotten the same processors as wedding gifts and theirs worked fine, but everyone has different circumstances. In fact, if some of her friends still have their machines, whilst others had to pass on unused ones to their *nands*, or part ways with their processors because they settled in the other corner of the world. Point being, *machines and marriages cannot be compared*. Everyone has their own deal breakers and makers. In the case of khala, it was a shared responsibility—a mix of overlooked technical needs and personal pride that led to the premature end of her food processor.

One needs to comprehend the set of circumstances one is in, and understand her man inside out, before complaining. This is the first step to knowing if a man can be fixed or not. Following the reasonable demands of your man, figuring out the triggers that lead to problems, and showing him that you're doing your part, can lead most men to do theirs. A little patience and a lot of understanding can completely alter your man and your marriage.

I know some women might hesitate to take the initiative or feel it's not their place to make the first move in solving issues. However, good men, when loved and nurtured properly, can blossom into wonderful husbands. It's important to remember that it's likely their first time handling this part of life as well.

There are a set of rules that, if applied, can help your man become a better husband to you:

The first step is *tareef*—a truly magnificent and cost-free action. Shower praise on your man at home, especially in front of the little eyes and ears that look up to both of you. When you tell your children that their *abu* is a wonderful person, that they're blessed to have a father who loves and protects them, it boosts his ability to lead them with confidence and authority. And if there aren't any children, focus on the things that your man does for you, more than the things he doesn't, and praise him for doing those. *Tareef* makes one accomplish the biggest things.

The second step is to speak well of him when you do speak of him. I understand that he might not be the best husband on the planet, but a lot of problems arise because women want to look down upon their better halves in front of their parents on issues such as finances, attire, behavior and so on. The disagreement may fade overnight and you'll reconcile with Faisal, but your parents' perception may remain altered. As for sharing the details with your *sahelis*, please don't. You could have the greatest female bond of all time, but discussing your bedroom details and the fact that he is too broke to purchase that leather bag every Phase 6 visiting woman has, is not nice. Your friend cannot make him get the bag or spice up your life with National *masala* hampers, so there's no benefit of ridiculing your better half during a *much needed BFF session.* Female friendships are precious, but they shouldn't come at the cost of your spouse's reputation. Similarly, some women who for the want of fitting in, make out their Faisal to be someone he's not. This sets unrealistic and unattainable standards that mislead naive women. And while it's wonderful to praise a deserving Faisal, *doing so excessively can invite envy and negativity.* Celebrate him modestly and keep some of your admiration between the two of you—it's safer and sweeter that way. There also exist women who keep quiet, but have the saddest expressions on their faces when questioned about their husbands. Now, this is not because their husbands are cruel, but because these women cannot be happy for long and want the next best thing in life to change that frown upside down. Don't do that. We all like to think we're judged on our own merits, but let's face it: how folks see you does rub off on your spouse. When you carry yourself with grace, kindness, and a touch of class around town, it doesn't just boost your image—it gives his a good shine too. Let your demeanor reflect the respect and love you have for your partner, ensuring it casts a glow that extends to him as well.

The third step to nurturing a stronger bond with your man is to wholeheartedly support his vision. Now, you may not entirely agree with that vision, but for the part that you do agree with, back it wholeheartedly. It's more than just nodding along when he talks about his dreams—be it starting his own showroom next to a hundred showrooms or teaching chess to children after office hours for free. Show genuine interest and chip in with ideas or solutions when he hits a roadblock. Celebrate the little wins along the way, and let him know you're his biggest fan. By investing in his dreams, you're not just fueling his drive—you're strengthening the foundation of your partnership. There might be moments when his dreams seem a bit far-fetched, but instead of dismissing them, respond with an encouraging *"One day, InshAllah."* Trust that he's aware of the challenges ahead, but dreams are vital for keeping one's spirit alive. Dreaming big is not a flaw—it's a glimpse of his ambition and hope, and nurturing that with kindness rather than skepticism can help strengthen your bond.

Faisal could be aspiring about having his father retire early, or building his *ama jee* her dream kitchen. Don't snap at him and tell him to think about you and his children first. Instead, tell him how wonderful it would be for aunty and uncle once all of this comes true. And even if it takes time, how lucky they are to have such a considerate son. Then, gently introduce your shared dreams that involve the whole family, suggesting that he can extend his care to being both; a considerate son and a considerate father. If Faisal is a good man, he will very well know the art of balance.

The fourth step is to nudge him gently towards spirituality. A man who fears Allah will not hurt your heart. Such a man is guided by wisdom and compassion, traits that can only enrich a marriage. It's not just about praying at the mosque, but about embedding those teachings in everyday life. It's important to recognize that not all who pray regularly practice what they preach. I have seen men who pray five times a day but hit their wives and step on the tails of cats, and refuse to give their daughters their shares. But I've also seen men who *understand the meaning of prayer,* and as they bow down to *sujood,* they do so to repent and become the best versions of themselves. A man who truly comprehends the words of God cannot belittle a woman. In fact, such a man can only treat her like a queen and nothing else.

The fifth step is to become a pillow filling. Perhaps the

one with duck feathers from Chenone. Create a haven for him at home. The world outside is harsh—filled with demanding people, economic challenges given the horrific conditions of Pakistan, and never-ending societal turmoil. Faisal needs to come home to a smiling wife and the aroma of his favorite *sabzi* simmering on the stove. Faisal *could* also pick his wife from work on his way back and the both of them could order in whilst his wife would set the plates and he would help wash them afterwards. The bottom line is that after a long day fighting the world, Faisal should not have to fight his wife.

Now that we've gone through the steps to help fix Faisal, let's talk about having a Faisal who cannot be fixed. The irreparable, thoughtless kind who, despite the efforts, still ridicules his wife, lacks empathy, lies compulsively, begrudges spending on his family, and in-short makes his wife wish that getting run over by a bus is a better option than spending another night with him. In such circumstances, it is important to understand that this version of Faisal might need to be let go. Do not be aunty Zubaida's daughter with two MPhils who said that God chose Faisal for her and so God will help her. God only helps those who help themselves. You don't rush to the prayer mat when you fall off the stairs and your head splits open. You run to the ER and get the proper treatment and then ask God to heal the wound. Similarly, dealing with a toxic relationship requires decisive action. *Dua (prayers) and Duwa (medicine) go hand in hand.* If you find yourself with a Faisal who shows no signs of change, do what's necessary for your well-being and peace of mind and then place the outcome in God's hands, knowing that you've done your part. Remember, no matter how many times you read a book, the ending is always the same.

———

Dear Ayesha,

Imagine marriage as a house—a place meant to be safe and warm. In every house, there's an exit door. For those fortunate enough to be with a 'fixable Faisal,' that door remains unseen, hidden behind the joy and contentment that fills their home. However, for those caught in endless strife, where each day with Faisal brings more sorrow than happiness, the exit is all too clear. Yet, they may obscure it with a sofa, crowd it with lush plants, or cover it with a collage of sparse happy memories. These women are caging themselves. Escaping an unhealthy marriage isn't the end of the world; in fact, it might just be the beginning. Outside that house, there's a whole world that could be far better than anything they've known inside.

Love, *the jinns.*

Chapter 3

Inter-sanctioned Relations

*Inter-sanctioned relations:
This chapter delves into the complex dynamics with South Asian in-laws, where interactions sometimes mirror diplomatic and economic sanctions. These "sanctions" can be imposed on the *bahu* (daughter-in-law) throughout her married life, influencing everything from social privileges to household responsibilities. [On some occasions, the husband can be sanctioned as well.]

**This section explores the nuances of these relationships and offers strategies for handling the often tricky waters of familial diplomacy.

Before we delve deeper, it's crucial for those not yet married to understand the importance of knowing your in-laws and the environment of the home you'll be entering, whether you'll live with them or not. These relationships can deeply impact your shaadi, sometimes working miracles to save unions that seemed doomed, or unfortunately, contributing to the breakdown of relationships that might have otherwise thrived. This initial awareness can be pivotal.

Tying the knot isn't just about uniting with your husband; it often means figuring out your place within a whole new family dynamic. Let's face it—everyone's on their best behavior until the ink dries on the marriage certificate. Once the festivities settle down, you might find that the congenial faces reveal more complex personalities. It's not uncommon to transition from being chummy with your future mother-in-law to suddenly finding yourself handling a tricky truce, all because you dared to establish a simple boundary post-nuptials. (It could be as simple as refusing to unlock your door after midnight.) Alternatively, you might be one of the fortunate few who find a second family in their in-laws, sometimes forming bonds even stronger than those with your own family.

Unfortunately, I've noticed that some women spend more time agonizing over choosing a lawn suit on sale with a mediocre tulip print than they do getting to know their soon-to-be family. While it's unlikely that your in-laws will fit neatly into one specific category, chances are you'll spot familiar traits in at least one of them! From the overly protective *saas* to the ever-interfering *susar*, knowing the type you're dealing with can smooth your integration into the family.

Handling the tricky world of Pakistani in-laws can sometimes feel like picking out the right spice for your biryani—it's crucial to get the mix just right. Here are some common types of Pakistani in-laws you might encounter, each with their unique flavor:

The "Our-Tehzeeb-Is-Everything" In-Laws:
This family runs a tight ship, mirroring a military general. Their home is their barracks where discipline is paramount. Expect schedules for meals, prayers, and even leisure. Charming yet commanding, they believe in the old adage, "my way or the

highway." Aligning with them might just mean adopting their meticulous timetable and it's the only way to settle-in. Bushra, a dear friend with this set of in-laws had to make a significant adjustment there because she came from a rather relaxed family. However, over time she realized that none of what was asked for was unfair in any aspect. If she had to serve food, it would only be to her husband not to the other six men in the house. If she had to stay awake after Fajar, it was because the entire house was up and she wasn't expected to do anything that others weren't.

Adjusting to life with such in-laws means getting a firm grasp on their expectations first and foremost. Timekeeping is a big deal in their book, so punctuality is your new best friend—being on time for meals, gatherings, and daily chores will earn you biryani points. Don't hesitate to step up and organize—whether it's planning the week's meals or tidying up. It shows you're not just participating but taking charge where you can. Remember to honor their traditions and the way things are done around the house. If some rules seem too stiff, find a calm moment to express your thoughts respectfully, showing you value their ways but also have your comfort to consider. You might want to openly communicate with your husband first. *Him being on your side is crucial.* It also might help to connect with other family members who've walked this path before—they can offer valuable insights and support as you find your footing. But tread carefully—not everyone may have your best interests at heart, and you wouldn't want to stir up a new *salan*. It's an open secret that the oldies love that; it's not a sure fact, but most relish seeing you go through the trouble they did. Most importantly, give yourself time to adapt. It's a shift, not just in routine but in mindset, and that doesn't happen overnight. Be easy on yourself and allow the process to unfold naturally. Keep a firm grip on your own well-being and identity. Yes, adapting is crucial, but it's equally important to safeguard your inner peace and sense of self. Remember, it's entirely possible—and absolutely essential—to stay true to who you are.

The "Production House" In-Laws:
Imagine every family gathering scripted like a prime-time Pakistani drama series—yes, that's the Drama Producer in-laws for you. These maestros of mayhem thrive on the highs and lows of domestic life, turning even the smallest misunderstanding into a three-episode saga. They have a flair for magnifying minor issues into prime-time-worthy crises. Whether it's the slightly overcooked roti or a misplaced dupatta, every incident is potential fodder for a family crisis, complete with dramatic pauses and teary confrontations. Buckle up, because, with them, you're in for a melodramatic ride.

Dealing with Production House in-laws requires the finesse of a seasoned diplomat. First, learn the art of setting boundaries. It's like drawing a *lakir* (line) with a bold marker—clear and visible. Decide what personal spaces and topics are off-limits, and communicate these boundaries calmly yet firmly. When the drama ensues, know when to respond and when to let the silence speak. Not every battle needs to be fought; sometimes, letting the storm pass without your input is the best reaction.

Involving your husband is essential but do it wisely. Share your feelings without making it seem like daily complaints that might make him dread coming home. Frame discussions around how maintaining harmony at home is beneficial for both of you. Remember, you're both on the same team.

If the theatrical antics become overwhelming, consider more drastic measures like seeking a separate living arrangement. If moving to a new house isn't immediately feasible, perhaps a separate portion within the same house could work. This isn't just about physical space—it's about preserving your mental peace and privacy. This gives everyone enough room to breathe and thus, reduces the chances of those dramatic clashes.

Adopting these strategies can help you maintain your sanity amidst the soap opera swirl. Understand that sometimes the best audience is the one that watches quietly, claps politely, and leaves the drama on the stage (or in this case, the living room) where it belongs.

The "Mighty Mughal" In-Laws:
Stepping into a family of business moguls means entering a world where high achievement isn't just appreciated; it's expected. In this family, WhatsApp groups buzz not only with discussions about dead presidents but also with spirited debates about relatives whose failure to pass the CSS exams marks them as 'dead' to the family's lofty ambitions. This is a clan where nothing is ever quite good enough, where every dinner might turn into a strategy session, and where expectations hover like hawks over every life choice. Expect your *dewar* (brother-in-law) to pitch startup ideas over dinner, and your *jethani* (elder brother's wife) to scrutinize your fashion choices for market potential. This family believes themselves to be the experts in anything and everything.

Take Laiba, for instance, a *bahu* in such a family, who found herself perpetually under scrutiny because her son wasn't enrolled in Aitchison College, one of the most prestigious schools in the country. Laiba faced daily taunts and was ridiculed for not meeting the family's stratospheric standards.

Dealing with a Business Mogul family requires a sturdy backbone and a strategic mind. They might belittle those who aren't versed in their fields of expertise or who don't share their appetite for relentless achievement. The trick to surviving—and thriving—in this environment is multifaceted.

Stepping into a family of business moguls is like walking into a never-ending board meeting, where every detail of your life is scrutinized. It can feel suffocating when every little thing from your parenting skills to your general knowledge is under constant review. For instance, imagine the stress if you're expected to have your toddler reciting the alphabet practically before he can walk, or plotting out his path to medical school while he's still in diapers.

The intensity only ramps up if your spouse is cut from the same cloth as his high-powered family. Suddenly, you're expected to match his mother's meticulous cleaning standards, his sister's culinary prowess, and maintain an appearance as flawless as his best friend, Salman's wife, who famously shed her postpartum weight faster than a season change, and Salman did not have to witness her flabby belly.

In such a high-pressure situation, setting boundaries is very important. It's important to have frank discussions with your spouse about the need for a balanced life, where your family's emotional well-being is as much a priority as living up to external expectations. Suggest practical steps like designating times or spaces in the home that are work-free zones, allowing you and your family to unwind and connect on a more personal level.

If the environment becomes too overwhelming despite these efforts, consider the benefits of more physical separation. Perhaps a nearby but separate living arrangement could provide the necessary breathing room while keeping familial connections intact.

And if things remain unbearable, and it feels like your personal growth and mental health are at stake, it might be necessary to contemplate *a more permanent separation*. It's a hard decision, but ultimately, preserving your own well-being is vital. In a family where the corporate mentality overshadows individual relationships, sometimes stepping away is the healthiest move to find peace and thrive.

The "Son-in-Womb" In-Laws

Stepping into a marriage with the "Son-in-the-Womb" in-laws is like entering a world where the umbilical cord was never cut. In these families, the son, whether he's the golden child or the baby of the brood, is babied to an extent that stifles his growth. He's not necessarily narcissistic; rather, he's so coddled and micro-managed by his parents that he struggles to make the simplest decisions on his own. In such households, the son might as well still be swaddled in the nursery for all the independence he's allowed.

This isn't a tell-tale sign but in majority of the cases, the son is the only child, or the only male child or the youngest child of the lot. Take, for instance, a family where the son is treated more like a delicate heirloom than a functioning adult. From picking out his clothes and deciding his meals to orchestrating his daily schedule, his parents control every thread of his life. If this son is married, don't expect a typical husband-wife dynamic. The in-laws are so enmeshed in their son's life that they might as well join the couple on their honeymoon—and if they can't physically be there, they're ringing in on video calls, ensuring their presence is felt around the clock.

Dealing with this type of family dynamic requires a strategy akin to walking a tightrope. If you find yourself married to such a "son-in-the-womb," recognize that no amount of affection or effort on your part is likely to wean him off his parental dependence. The relationship between you and your husband can be perpetually overshadowed by the overbearing love of his parents.

For *bahus* caught in this suffocating embrace, there are a few survival tactics. First and foremost, establishing clear boundaries about personal space and couple time is essential, although this may mean initiating some tough conversations with your husband about the necessity of weaning off constant parental oversight. Additionally, seeking external support through counseling or a supportive friend network can provide not only emotional relief but also practical advice for handling the situation. Encouraging your husband towards small acts of independence—like deciding on weekend plans or managing personal appointments—can gradually bolster his confidence and autonomy. However, if the dynamics remain stifling and show no signs of improvement, it's crucial to consider your own mental health and well-being. In such cases, contemplating an exit strategy might become necessary, not just for your own sanity but also for a healthier future. Remember, staying in an overwhelming environment is not obligatory, and sometimes, stepping back to regain your happiness and independence is the healthiest decision you can make.

The *"Lain Dain"* In-Laws

Introducing the "Lain-Dain In-Laws," masters of the art of give-and-take, but with a twist that leans heavily on the 'give'—from your side, of course! In their world, the tradition of dowry is dressed up as 'gifts of love' for the daughter's happiness. These aren't just any gifts; we're talking about the full spectrum—from swanky kitchen appliances to perhaps even a house—all in the name of ensuring she lives a life of luxury.

And let's not forget the gold for occasions that also remember those who have long left us. Yes, these in-laws keep the goldsmiths busy even in remembrance of deceased relatives! Despite these glaring red flags, many women find themselves unable to escape, bogged down by societal pressures, the ticking biological clock, or simply because they believe this is what every family does to secure a daughter's future.

For those who walk down the aisle with these families, the giving never stops. It's an endless stream of outflows that you're expected to maintain till your last breath. Handling the "Lain-Dain" in-laws is no walk in the park. Recognizing these early signs is crucial: if wedding talks feel more like corporate deals loaded with inventory lists, you might want to rethink your steps.

Let's spin the tale of Tazeen, whose journey as a new bride felt more like managing a minefield of critical in-laws than walking down the aisle. She constantly faced snide remarks about the inadequacy of her dowry and the supposedly questionable behavior of her family at social events. Thankfully, her husband was her steadfast ally, always ready to diffuse the tension and shield her from the family drama.

However, the dynamic took a sharp turn when her devrani arrived flaunting a brand new Honda Civic. Instantly, Tazeen found herself sidelined, criticized not for what she brought to the table, but for what she didn't—a car, despite the family already owning three. The audacity was staggering. It could have been the breaking point for Tazeen if fate hadn't dealt a more favorable hand. Her husband received a German visa, and just like that, they were off to a new life miles away from the unwarranted critiques.

Now, with continents between them, Tazeen enjoys her peace. She flatly refuses to host her in-laws and only deals with their drama biennially. Living abroad has given her the breathing space she desperately needed, proving sometimes a little distance is the best solution to maintaining one's sanity in the face of relentless family pressure.

The "Second Family" In-Laws

Meet the "Second Family In-Laws," those rare gems who turn the often-feared in-law relationship into a heartwarming chapter straight out of a feel-good novel. They welcome their *bahu* with the warmth and affection typically reserved for a daughter returning home. Mistakes? They're met with understanding and forgiveness. Achievements? Celebrated as if they were their own. Privacy is a given, not a battleground, making the new family dynamic refreshingly respectful.

The special part about such in-laws is that they understand the *bahu* is like a daughter, but not wholly their daughter, so there's always a line of boundaries that cannot be crossed. This is beautiful if you think about it; you enjoy the perks of being a daughter but understand the reality that you're not a blood relation, so the expectations are not unrealistic and healthy boundaries are always intact, which fosters love.

However, it's important for a woman to recognize that if she is blessed with such in-laws, it's only fair to reciprocate and treat them like her own family. *Rishtas* like these are delicate, often hanging by a thread—years of love and affection can be tarnished in the blink of an eye. Thus, nurturing these bonds with care and mutual respect is crucial to maintaining a harmonious family life.

There's a cautionary note for women who might be so swept up in the lavish love showered by their in-laws that they turn a blind eye to any mistreatment from their husbands. It's essential to remember that while having supportive in-laws is a significant blessing, their kindness should never be a veil that obscures the actions of a troublesome Faisal. At the end of the day, when all retreat to their corners of the world, you're the one who has to share the quiet of the night with him. And often, those silent nights can stretch into endless, lonely days when no one else is around to witness what unfolds behind closed doors. In such times, the affection of in-laws, no matter how genuine, cannot compensate for a partnership that drains your spirit. Always remember, self-care isn't selfish—it's necessary. So, make sure you're not just surviving but thriving in your marriage, by putting yourself first, always.

The "Ex" In-Laws

Meet the "Ex" In-Laws—the type of relatives who turn the matrimonial journey into a never-ending nightmare. These in-laws come with traits that could darken any doorstep: cruelty, manipulation, and narcissism are just the start. And, as outlandish as it might sound, some have even been tied to secretive, cult-like activities within posh neighbourhoods like DHA. Regrettably, this isn't just fodder for dramatic gossip; it's a grim reality for some unfortunate *bahus*.

With such in-laws, no amount of patience, reassurance, or sabr can salvage the *bahu*'s well-being. Sometimes the toxicity may stem from just one individual, but often, that one person can cast such a long shadow that any residual goodness is completely overshadowed. It's in these extreme cases that staying becomes more detrimental than leaving. These in-laws are the very epitome of regrettable mistakes, and they underscore why, although divorce is generally frowned upon, it remains a justified, permissible option in our religion.

Cutting ties with such oppressive in-laws might feel like you're facing the apocalypse, but in truth, it's far from it. It's an escape, a much-needed liberation from a toxic environment. While it may seem daunting at first, removing yourself from their influence is not just good riddance—it's a vital step towards reclaiming your peace and paving the way for a healthier future. Sometimes, ending one chapter is the only way to begin another, hopefully on a path that leads to happiness and healing.

It's clear that the realm of in-laws is as varied as it is vibrant.

Each encounter is more than just a chapter in a book; it's a real-life saga filled with its own drama, laughter, and sometimes, tears.

Dealing with this mixed bag of in-laws is like perfecting your chai brewing technique—knowing when to simmer the spices and when to add just enough sugar to balance the bitterness. It's about stirring in a bit of humor, a dash of patience, and a whole lot of savvy to keep the peace without losing your own spice.

———

Dear Ayesha,

In the play of the in-laws, sometimes you lead, sometimes you follow, and sometimes, dear Ayesha, you simply step aside and enjoy the music. Today, you handle the maze of in-laws, but remember, the wheel of time spins swiftly; one day post Maghrib, you will find yourself on the other side of the door, holding the keys to the rashan pantry, as the saas of your son's wife.

Consider this a gentle reminder from the jinns who've seen countless cycles of the moon: the roles we play today are but rehearsals for the roles we inherit tomorrow. Many a bahu, who once trembled at the sound of her saas's footsteps, finds herself echoing those very steps. It is the way of the world, the play of generations.

But here lies the rub — and the opportunity. Armed with the memories of your own zindagi, you have the power to change the tune. When the day comes for you to welcome someone new into your family fold, remember the feelings, the fears, and the wishes you harbored. You can be the change. You must.

Love, the jinns.

Chapter 4

Treasuring Tariq

Welcome to Chapter 4, where we delve into the evolving art of cherishing the man you vowed to spend your life with—your husband, your partner, your Tariq. Love, as they say, is a verb, and in the context of marriage, it's an action that must be renewed each day after Fajr. This chapter is about how to love your husband when you first get married, how to love your husband when you've been married for ten years and how to love your husband on days where you have no love to give.

Aadmi loug are indeed creatures of deep emotion, often moved deeply by the simple, tender gestures that thread through daily life. Consider how a spontaneous hug or a lingering kiss can light up Tariq's face, how a smile from across the room can pull him closer, or how a heartfelt thank you after a long day can melt away his worries. These moments, small as they may seem, are potent signals of affection and appreciation that resonate deeply within a man's heart.

For example, imagine Tariq coming home tired from work, the weight of his day evident in his slumped shoulders and furrowed brow. Now picture the transformation when you greet him with a warm embrace and a bright smile, acknowledging his hard work, despite having had a hard day with his *ama jee* at home. It's not just temporary comfort you're offering; it's a deep recognition of his efforts and his worth. The rants of how your day went can wait.

Men often build their emotional connections through the tactile, feeling love not just in their hearts but in their very *skin*. While women may need emotional intimacy to open the doors to physical closeness, men might feel more emotionally intertwined as physical intimacy deepens. This is a very important reality to understand.

Take, for instance, a quiet evening where Tariq is trying to unwind after a taxing day at work. As you sit beside him, you casually reach out and take his hand in yours, or perhaps you gently massage his shoulders. These physical touches act as conduits for emotional connection.

This tactile connection can be deeply grounding for men like Tariq. While you might seek a conversation to feel closer, Tariq finds that same closeness when you simply share a couch, your legs entwined while you both watch reels. It's in these moments of shared silence and subtle touches that he often feels most loved and connected.

Let's consider Tariq during a season where things aren't quite going as planned—perhaps the bonus didn't come through or a new job opportunity fell through. These are the moments that really test the fabric of your relationship. How you communicate with him during these times becomes crucial. Addressing Tariq with warmth and understanding, especially when the chips are down, can reinforce his confidence and affirm your partnership. And, it's not just about what you say, but how you say it. Choosing words that uplift rather than critique—focusing on his efforts and the hard work he's put in, rather than the disappointing outcome—shows that you see and appreciate all of him, not just his successes. This kind of supportive dialogue is what builds a fortress around your relationship, shielding it from the storms of doubt and insecurity. For days when you're not yourself, Tariq will recall the moments when you were.

Imagine the meaningful impact of saying, "I see how hard you're trying, and that means everything to me," instead of pointing out how his sister visits her *maika* four times a week and Tariq isn't providing enough to feed her and her Sufi-tenders loving children.

Men and women often handle stress in distinctly different ways, which can sometimes lead to misunderstandings in how they support each other during tough times. Take Tariq, for instance, who might respond to stress by becoming quieter, immersing himself in work, or finding solace in solitude. This is a common response among many men who are more inclined to process their stress internally rather than expressing it outwardly. They might retreat, distract themselves, or even appear to ignore the issue at hand as a way to cope.

On the other hand, consider how you might handle stress differently. Like many women, perhaps you find it therapeutic to express your emotions and talk through your challenges. You might seek to connect with Tariq, wanting to share your feelings and seeking comfort in the verbal expression of your stress.

The challenge arises when Tariq's instinct to withdraw clashes with your need to communicate. During such times, you might feel isolated or rejected just when you need support the most, while Tariq might feel pressured to engage in conversations that feel uncomfortable or forced, adding to his stress rather than alleviating it.

Understanding these differing approaches to stress can greatly impact how you support each other. Recognizing that Tariq's quietness isn't a rejection but a personal coping mechanism can help you give him the space he needs. Meanwhile, Tariq acknowledging your need to talk things through can lead him to provide a listening ear, even if it's just to offer reassurance before he takes time to himself. This mutual respect for each other's coping strategies not only prevents feelings of neglect or pressure but also strengthens your bond by fostering deeper empathy and support.

Now, let's talk about the Platinum Rule of Relationships—it's a real game changer. While the Golden Rule tells us to treat others how we'd like to be treated, the Platinum Rule shifts the focus a bit: treat Tariq the way he wants to be treated. It's a simple tweak that can bring huge improvements to your relationship.

Think about it this way: Tariq might really feel loved when you show admiration for his work or when you're openly proud of his accomplishments or simply when you laugh at his not-so-funny jokes. So, even if you personally value cuddles and gifts more, recognizing what makes Tariq tick is key.

For example, if Tariq lights up when you support his hobby of photography, show interest. He might not be earning from it. In fact, the hobby might be time-consuming and not so cost-effective. But, ask him about his latest shots, suggest a weekend photo outing, or maybe frame one of his pictures as a surprise. It shows you care about what's important to him.

By applying the Platinum Rule, you're not just going through the motions of a relationship; you're actively enhancing it by ensuring that your actions resonate deeply with Tariq. This approach doesn't just keep the peace; it deepens the love and respect between you.

Understanding what "love" truly means to your partner is essential, yet it's often overlooked.

Remember, every man is unique and thus, some women don't know for sure what makes their Tariq feel most loved. The simplest approach is often just to ask him. Open, honest communication can uncover insights that you might not discover otherwise.

Sometimes in life, we discover that not every Tariq is meant to be held close. Some Tariqs are meant to be loved from afar. Despite pouring your heart into the relationship, there are times when it feels like you're trying to unlock a door with no key. Just like a *pista* sealed without a crack, some hearts aren't meant to be opened by your efforts alone.

Let me tell you about my dear friend Aimen's elder sibling who lives in Qatar. She was once married to a man in Pakistan. Her then-husband was born and bred in the UAE, and he settled in Pakistan for business purposes. From the very beginning, the relationship was a troubled one. Despite having spent time together before marriage, their relationship soured dramatically after the wedding, and their troubles were attributed to black magic, a common scapegoat in South Asian culture. Now, the dark arts very much exist - there's no denying that. Envious women and men destroy their *emaan* and the lives of others. But that's the story for another time. Coming back to Aimen's sibling - she would diligently recite the *azkar*, which again, one should. She believed that any lapse in her daily spiritual protections led directly to chaos in her home. However, after two years of turmoil, she came to the realization that her struggles were not due to *kaala jaadu* or her husband being possessed by a jinn. The truth was much simpler yet harder to accept: that she was just married to a horrid individual who was not capable of loving her.

It's essential to recognize the signs that your love isn't landing as it should. Maybe Tariq rarely initiates contact, always claiming busyness, or he doesn't seem to prioritize time with you, leaving you feeling more like an option than a priority. Perhaps interactions that should be intimate feel transactional, or worse, you feel unseen and unheard, even in moments of vulnerability.

Consider this: if Tariq seems detached during your most challenging times, if he mocks or neglects your needs, or if your efforts at nurturing the relationship feel one-sided, these are strong indicators that the emotional investment isn't mutual. Love, in its truest form, is a two-way street.

If you find yourself continually justifying his lack of connection or making excuses for his absence in key moments, it might be time to step back. Loving Tariq from a distance isn't about giving up on love; it's about respecting yourself enough to recognize that true affection should not be one-sided.

So, if you're facing a love that feels locked away behind an impenetrable shell, remember that your well-being and happiness are paramount. Sometimes, the bravest act of love is to walk away, not with bitterness, but with the hope and openness to one day find a connection that truly reciprocates your depth of feeling.

———

Dear Ayesha,

Sometimes there's another possibility. You and Tariq might do everything right—care for each other, support each other, share laughter and dreams—but it still won't work out. It might feel something indefinable is missing or worse, it may feel as if nothing is missing at all and that you both are meant for each other and yet, it still won't work out. It's like planting two beautiful flowers side by side in the same pot, only to find they don't thrive.

This doesn't mean there's anything wrong with either of you. It's just that sometimes, good people aren't meant to be good together. Remember, two people might be good, but they might be bad for each other. It could be the timing, the environment, or simply the mysterious ways of fate.

When love doesn't flourish the way you hoped, remember, it's not a reflection of your worth or his. It's just life's way of saying there might be a different path for each of you where you'll bloom more fully.

Remember, parting ways doesn't take away the good times you've shared or the genuine affection you felt. It's simply an acknowledgment that you both deserve to be happy, even if that happiness isn't found together.

Love, *the jinns.*

Chapter 5

Loving Lubna

Welcome to Chapter 5 - your guide to reminding your man why falling in love with you isn't just a one-time event, but a daily discovery. My *nano* always said every woman is an unfolding story, a mystery to be unraveled, and a journey worth taking again and again. This chapter is about making sure Tariq remembers that every day.

Sometimes after the *nikkah* is done and the title of *new dulhan* settles, your once-lit world starts to flicker. Remember, though, that shaadi isn't the finish line; it's the starting gate. Keeping Tariq enchanted shouldn't be a task relegated to the courtship phase—it's a lifelong endeavor.

Be a mystery movie: Just because Tariq now shares your last name doesn't mean he should know your every thought and move. Surprise him! Make his favorite curry *chawal* that takes ages to make, gift him the bread kit he's had his eyes on, or have the children go to bed early to catch up in silence. These little mysteries keep the intrigue alive, reminding Tariq of the days when every *mulaqat* brought a new revelation about the incredible woman he chose to marry.

Have a separate zindagi: Showing that you have a life outside of the relationship makes you more attractive and allows the relationship to breathe. Nothing rekindles interest like seeing someone passionately engaged in their own interests. Whether it's painting, yoga, or a cook club, keep up with your hobbies. Tariq will adore seeing you glow with enthusiasm. Plus, it gives you both something exciting to share and discuss during your together time.

Make curry but don't smell like it: In the whirlwind of daily life, it's easy to reserve your best outfits for social outings, slipping into comfort mode at home. Every so often, throw on that dress that made Tariq's heart skip a beat or the perfume that reminds him of your first date. It's not about vanity; it's about showing Tariq he's worth the effort, every single day. And this will make him think about you at all times.

Embrace your flaws: Maintaining a perfect, goody-two-shoes facade in your relationship isn't just exhausting—it can actually backfire. Being perpetually on your best behavior might make you seem more like a superhero than a human to Tariq, and let's face it, even Wonder Woman has her off days. Continuously portraying yourself as faultless can set an unrealistic standard and inadvertently make Tariq feel as though he's the only one with flaws in the relationship. Mehak Usman can make cookies, knit bed sheets, and make *masalas* at home and we're really happy for her, but sometimes she burns the cookies and the bedsheets aren't according to the measurements and the *masalas* don't turn out as expected and she does everything and just about anything to not let anyone find out. Oh, dear.

Here's the thing, Lubna: it's okay to let Tariq see that you're not always the paragon of virtue. Maybe it's letting him see you binge-watch your guilty pleasure TV shows, skip a workout, or enjoy that extra slice of cake. These moments of 'imperfection' are incredibly humanizing and relatable. These are the times that show him you're comfortable enough with him to be your true self—quirks, indulgences, and all. Embrace the notion that a little edge can add spice to your relationship. It keeps things dynamic and interesting, reminding Tariq that being in love with you is never dull.

Keep the bedroom alive: Keeping the bedroom spark alive in your marriage is essential. Remember, intimacy and sexual attraction are foundational to a thriving relationship. Tariq, like many men, is visually stimulated, and staying visually appealing is a key part of maintaining the spark. But beyond just looking good, it's important to keep evolving sexually. Continuously exploring each other's desires and fantasies can keep the intimacy exciting and vibrant. Don't shy away from experimenting with new ideas or revisiting ones that have worked in the past.

For example, consider scheduling a regular 'date night' that focuses on rekindling your physical connection. Transform your bedroom into a sensual retreat with soft lighting, inviting scents, and perhaps some seductive music. These nights are not just about being physically intimate; they're about reinforcing the emotional and physical bonds that drew you to each other in the first place.

Know that mutual satisfaction is key: Do note it's crucial *that both Lubna and Tariq find fulfillment and joy in sex.* Just as Tariq's confidence blooms when he knows he can satisfy Lubna, it's equally important for Lubna to truly experience pleasure and connection in their intimate moments. It's a shared dance where both partners deserve to see the stars.

Lubna, being open and honest about what you need in bed

is not just beneficial—it's necessary. Communication is the key to a mutually satisfying intimate relationship. It's important to gently express your desires and preferences. Let Tariq know what feels good, what you'd like more of, or what new things you might want to explore together.

Avoid the trap of faking satisfaction. While it might seem like a shortcut to boost Tariq's ego, it can lead to long-term dissatisfaction for you.

Ask Tariq to fetch some yogurt: The Ben Franklin Effect is a fascinating psychological phenomenon that suggests a person's affection for you can actually increase after they do you a favor. Essentially, if Tariq does a favor for you, he might subconsciously justify his action by believing he did the favor because he likes you, thereby actually increasing his affection towards you.

Lubna is Mrs. Tariq: According to the Similarity/Attraction Theory, we are naturally drawn to individuals who mirror our own values, interests, and traits. This phenomenon suggests that demonstrating alignment with Tariq's beliefs and hobbies can significantly deepen your connection. For instance, if Tariq has a rebellious streak, sharing stories of your own adventurous escapades or expressing your non-conformist views can spark his interest and admiration. But don't be like Amina Ansari, who has a made-up story for having experienced everything in life. You want to interest Tariq, not eliminate his interest altogether. Similarly, if Tariq values family deeply, making it a point to discuss the importance of your own family ties and involving him in family gatherings can reinforce your shared values.

Talk to Tariq: When you lean in and ask Tariq for his thoughts or advice, you're doing more than just soliciting his opinion—you're telling him that he's important to you. Everyone likes to feel needed, and Tariq is no exception. This simple act can deepen his affection for you, as it underscores his significance in your decisions. Each time you consult him, whether it's on something big like picking a school for Abdullah or small like what type of *shaami kebab* to make for afternoon tea, you're reinforcing that his input is essential. It's these moments that subtly bind him more tightly into the fabric of your daily life.

Touching Tariq helps: When you're with Tariq, the power of touch can work wonders in conveying affection and building warmth between you two. Simple, gentle touches—a light caress on his back, a soft pat on his arm, a tender touch on his shoulder, or a playful nudge on his leg—these small gestures can significantly enhance his feelings of closeness to you. But of course, many Pakistani Tariqs cherish their morning and evening massages. Take the case of Alina Nasir. Whenever she leaves her apartment to spend the night with her parents, and the clock strikes six, Mr. W finds himself wishing she were back home. Alina has so positively reinforced her presence in her husband's life that even a minor leg ache reminds him of her absence, as amusing as that may sound.

Sshhh, Tariq! It's *our* secret: Letting Tariq in on a secret is like giving him a backstage pass to your life—it's intimate, it's exclusive, and it shows him he's special. When you lean in and whisper something in his ear that you haven't shared with anyone else, you're not just sharing information; you're building trust. It's like telling him, "Here's a piece of my heart that only you can see." This gesture makes him feel deeply valued and draws him closer to you, wrapping him in the warmth of being your confidant. Of course, there are Tariqs who, despite being decent husbands, seem to have sieve-like bellies that can't keep anything inside. Broadcasting their wives' secrets, often with a generous dash of exaggeration, is their favorite pastime.

Lubna's luscious curls matter: It might sound a bit unusual, but there's a fascinating aspect to how attraction works, especially when it comes to hair. Believe it or not, Tariq, like many men, may find himself drawn to shiny, clean, and longer hair without even realizing why. This preference isn't just about aesthetics; it's deeply rooted in evolutionary psychology. Historically, lush hair has been seen as a marker of health and fertility—qualities that were crucial when our ancestors chose partners.

Humor is the heartbeat of love: Injecting a dash of humor into your relationship with Tariq is like sprinkling a bit of *tarka* onto your *daal*—it enhances everything! Trust me, it's a myth that men don't value humor in women. In reality, Tariq will absolutely relish your witty side. It's not just about giggling at his jokes (though a genuine chuckle never hurts); it's about being someone who can light up the room with a quick, clever comment or a funny observation.

Picture this: You're both stuck in Lahore's never ending traffic, a situation ripe for frustration. Instead of a sigh, you crack a joke or remember a funny thing from the past. Suddenly, the mood shifts, and there's laughter where there might have been grumbling. That's the power of humor—it transforms moments, eases tension, and draws you closer, showing Tariq that life with you is not just bearable, but actually a lot of fun.

Life isn't just about sustaining Tariq's interest—it's about actively cultivating a rich, fulfilling relationship that continues to grow and surprise. It's about ensuring that every day Tariq wakes up, he has new reasons to fall in love with you all over again.

———

Dear Ayesha,

Every Lubna has a keen sense of her Tariq's affections, even if his way of showing love is not as loud or visible as others might express. Love isn't always about grand gestures or poetic words—it's often felt in the quiet, unspoken moments that resonate deep within. Trust this intuition, for even when love doesn't parade itself, it leaves a tangible warmth that's hard to miss.

But remember, dear Lubna, if there comes a time when you pause and ponder whether you deserve better, trust that inner voice. You should never feel lost in the effort to keep a love that refuses to blossom, nor should you diminish yourself for someone who might never truly cherish what you offer.

So, Lubna, if the day ever comes when love feels more like longing than fulfillment, close your eyes and know that letting go isn't a defeat; it's a deep, brave breath. Should you ever feel the pull to step away, know it's not abandoning what was but honoring what could be—for both of you.

Love, *the jinns.*

Chapter 6

Bedbugs on Blooming Bedsheets

In this chapter, we'll delve into the not-so-pleasant but essential topic of tackling the inevitable conflicts that creep into every marriage, much like uninvited bedbugs on beautiful bedsheets. We'll go through spine-chilling tales of marriages tested by the ghosts of the past and present. It's an exploration of whether old scars or current trials can irrevocably alter the fabric of a relationship—whether there's a way to mend what has been torn or if some cracks are indeed permanent. This narrative will guide you through stories that ponder if sometimes, the challenges and conflicts—our metaphorical bedbugs—might actually serve to strengthen bonds rather than just fray them.

In 2008, a young Conventarian whose parents were hardly home and in the midst of a messy divorce, fell in love with her van driver. She was the eldest sister of a friend, and we used to call her Bajo. Bajo, always more robust and hit by puberty earlier than her peers, faced cruel bullying at school for her acne, unruly frizzy hair that were uncontrollable in the heat, and the braces that framed her smile. This external chaos mirrored her internal turmoil: once a high achiever, her academic performance began to wane as she grappled with her appearance, the overt favoritism at school, and her increasingly absent parents. During this vulnerable time, Bajo formed an unlikely attachment to her van driver, a relationship I inadvertently witnessed as a young schoolmate. On days when her sister, my friend, was absent, Bajo would ask me to wait with her at the van, rewarding me with a Jet Sport for my company. It was during these moments that I saw Bajo, seeking solace, resting her head in the driver's lap, each time I looked up from my Enid Blyton book. When I once suggested she might be safer with my driver, she sharply rebuked me, insisting that I was too young to understand love. Anyway, the friend and I had a major fall out because she borrowed my glitter pens and did not return them and eventually I stopped seeing Bajo because she went to college. Years later, our paths crossed again at a university conference. Bajo, draped in a maroon chaddar too heavy for the season and looking markedly plain, spoke about climate change with a lack of passion that was palpable. Afterward, over reluctant tea, she revealed the unraveling of her own life post-college. She told me that she recently got divorced and lost custody of her two children. There was nothing wrong with her husband per se. In fact, it was a love marriage. However one night, amongst telling him other things, she had informed him about her relationship with the van driver, to which he had laughed, but then she had gone ahead and told him how they, the driver and Bajo, had once run away and Bajo's father had managed to bring her back after three days. Now, Bajo and her husband had a seemingly good life with two school-going children and she managed to unknowingly poison it. Because after that, her husband went on a verbal lockdown. The physical intimacy stopped. Her husband was unable to reconcile the woman he knew with her past. He couldn't put a finger on whether it was having a wife who had run away with a lover that was the problem or that the problem was the wife having almost been married to a van driver that repulsed him. Either way, the marriage took its course and died. She confided that she had hoped sharing her past would clear the air, but instead, it shattered her husband's perception of her. The disclosure, meant to lighten her burden, only added weight to their relationship, leading to a divorce and her losing custody of their children. Had what God intended to hide remained hidden, things would have been different. Bajo's story is a haunting reminder of the complexities of transparency within a marriage. While honesty is generally foundational, there are pasts so potent that they might be better left untouched—especially those capable of resurfacing and wreaking havoc on a present filled with promise.

Some people embrace a life mantra: once a decision is made, they stick to it, steadfast, even if whispers of doubt echo in their minds about its long-term wisdom. They commit to making it work, believing firmly in no backsies, no retreats. Then there are others who aren't necessarily bad people, but sometimes they make bad decisions or get swayed by bad influences, leading them to places they'd rather not be.

However, life has a way of showing us the true impact of our decisions only after we see the outcomes. Sometimes, even when a decision seems to bring happiness, there's a lingering feeling of loss. It's in these moments we realize that what we've won might not be as valuable as what we've lost:

Born into a prominent Indian family in 1968, Bee Begum dared to defy her family's expectations by marrying a man they dismissively called a "commoner." From the outset, her family tried to sour her views on her husband, warning her that their bloodlines should never mix. Despite the stark contrast between her affluent background, where she slept on mattresses larger than her lover's entire home, Bee Begum fought passionately for her love. It was a tough battle, one waged in the face of harsh opposition from her family who, entrenched in their beliefs about status and heritage, could not accept her choice. They even demanded a promise from her—a promise that she would never have children with her husband, believing that it would bring disgrace upon their lineage. But Bee Begum, ever the rebel, defied them once more. She not only continued to stand by her husband but also welcomed two beautiful children into the world, challenging the antiquated prejudices of her family and affirming her belief in the power of love over legacy. Her lover was a loving and caring man who went through all odds to care for his wife and children within the means that he had. When the twins turned twelve, Bee Begum got an opportunity to host a morning radio show. Her husband was her staunchest supporter and as she pursued what made her happy, he took the twins with him to work and looked after them.

Eventually, as Bee Begum's name grew in the public eye, she gained significant fame but not the financial success that often accompanies such recognition. Surrounded by people who flaunted their wealth, she began to feel a growing discomfort with her modest lifestyle, despite her husband's enduring support and the genuine happiness they had cultivated together. And that is when she put nineteen years of her husband's loyalty and hardship aside, she filed for divorce and returned to her affluent family, who accepted her with open arms, but their love for the twins remained tinged.

As the years passed, the allure of Bee Begum's morning radio show dimmed, eclipsed by the advent of grand television sets that captivated the audience in new and exciting ways. The twins, now living a life of luxury, slept on expensive mattresses and were tended to by maids, a stark contrast to their earlier, simpler life. Yet, despite the material comforts and the return to her family's affluence, Bee Begum felt an emptiness that luxury could not satiate. And so, Bee Begum returned to the village where she had lived with her husband, hoping to reconnect with the man who had once been her everything. However, when she arrived, her heart sank as she discovered that he had vanished without a trace.

When the husband found out that Bee Begum had come looking for him, he sent a message for her requesting her to not look for him and to remember all the lies she and her family spewed to keep the twins from meeting him. He further expressed a belief that, despite everything, Bee Begum was inherently a good woman. He trusted that she would fulfill the roles of both mother and father to their children. This message from her husband devastated Bee Begum. The weight of their fractured past and his resignation to a life apart from her and their children took a severe toll on her health. Despite her family's attempts to comfort her with claims that her husband had simply run off with someone more suited to his own social standing—a "commoner woman" like himself—Bee Begum knew the truth of his isolation and the deep wounds that their separation had inflicted upon both of them.

Her health deteriorated rapidly and the family's dismissive stories could not fill the void left by her husband's absence nor ease the guilt and regret that haunted her. It is said that Bee Begum died of a broken heart *and the burden of making a wrong decision.*

From a young age, my dear relative Adeel, never knew when to stop giving. As children, we cousins would commandeer his entire stash of Fruit Gala and Fanty candies, exploiting the strict rule set by his *ami* that he was allowed only one candy per day. In return, all he asked was that we include him in our games of *oonch neech*. As the years rolled on and our tastes evolved to Tic Tacs and Milk Duds, Adeel, ever eager to maintain his place in our circle, would have his brother-in-law procure these premium treats. He'd dash across the park with his latest acquisitions, a proud smile lighting up his face. By our teenage years, we began to suspect that Adeel's continued generosity might be driven by a crush on one of us, especially since he started offering rides to the academy. Yet, it wasn't just about the rides; Adeel was there for us unconditionally—tutoring us in statistics, enduring long queues under the blistering heat with the office help to submit our admission forms, and performing countless other errands. And *sheera* on top, he was the same to every individual we knew; which was why, sadly, to most, Adeel remained a background figure—always there, always helpful, but seldom truly seen. His unwavering kindness painted him as commonplace, an ever-present resource rather than a person with his own needs and desires.

Adeel, ever the giver in our family, married a distant cousin of ours who, frankly, seemed crafted on a Sunday—strikingly beautiful in a way that left people murmuring about Adeel's good fortune. Everyone said he had outdone himself, snagging such a catch; he was the lucky one, they declared. Yet beneath this enviable facade, his life was far from fortunate. Adeel's wife, however, quickly transformed their marriage into a battlefield. Their home was never their own, always overflowing with her relatives who treated it more like a free vacation spot than a newlywed's sanctuary. Her brothers and their wives would commandeer their bedroom for weeks on end, relegating Adeel to the couch in his own home. Worse still, she dictated who he could see and talk to, cutting him off from his own family and monitoring his every move online.

Despite witnessing the tumult he lived in, many of us, including his immediate family, resigned ourselves to the notion that Adeel had somehow chosen this life. Perhaps because he always adapted, always endured, we underestimated the depth of his misery. It was easier to believe that Adeel, who never complained and always bent to accommodate others, was somehow okay with his lot. This oversight allowed us to gloss over the harsh reality of his situation—that Adeel, the perennial giver, was trapped in a life where his generosity and good nature were being exploited to the breaking point.

Adeel's life slowly unfolded to us as a series of troubling whispers from friends who kept tabs on him. They said he had a child, although anyone passing by their house could spot two young kids playing in the yard. It turned out the other child was his sister-in-law's, who, for reasons unbeknownst to us, seemed to have moved in permanently.

As the years trickled by, Adeel's interactions with his own family became rarer and highly conditional, almost transactional. It was a heart-wrenching turn for someone who once freely gave everything of himself. The control his wife wielded over him tightened, morphing into outright aggression. Stories circulated that during her wilder outbursts, she would even resort to physical violence. Adeel, stuck in his ever-accommodating ways, bore it silently, trapped in a toxic loop that he couldn't—or wouldn't—escape. His plight deepened into a public spectacle when his wife was caught shoplifting abroad!

When we finally met Adeel's eight-year-old daughter, we were taken aback by her behavior, which starkly contrasted with the gentle nature of her father. Expecting a semblance of Adeel's kindness in her, we were instead greeted with a display of unchecked aggression; she spat in Adeel's face, hurled insults at a cousin over a pair of sunglasses that resembled her mother's, and in a fit of rage, snatched the sunglasses, scratching the cousin's nose in the process. The incident culminated in her smashing a bowl of nimko, all under the approving eye of her chuckling mother who seemed to validate her actions at every turn. Now, all that we witnessed was far from normal but at that time, we kept our (bruised) noses to ourselves.

At the start of 2024, Adeel finally reached his breaking point and decided to file for divorce. It wasn't that he couldn't keep up with the endless demands, like a gardener forever tending to an insatiable plant, but rather, he saw the detrimental effects this was having on the most delicate bloom of all—his daughter. In his heart, he knew that the relentless overwatering was causing her to wilt right before his eyes.

The court granted him custody for four days a week, a decision that brought his daughter into a new environment at her nano's house in Shadman. Initially resistant, she slowly began to accept her new reality, swayed by small tokens of affection like paid iPad apps—not an ideal solution, but a seed of a fresh start.

This decision was a stark departure from the Adeel we knew—the one who always bent before he would break. Yet, enduring the unrelenting strain without seeking change was no longer bearable. This decision marked a great shift for Adeel, the man who always leaned towards compromise rather than confrontation. These decisions, though heart-wrenching, are sometimes necessary. While the immediate aftermath might be painful, the alternative—continuing to endure a harmful situation—would be far more detrimental. Sometimes, the hardest decisions are not just choices but imperatives, and avoiding them can be even harder than facing them head-on.

If you sit down for a cup of chai with any nano, be it mine, yours, or one from the next street over, you'll likely hear a common wisdom: children save marriages. They'll say that a marriage without children teeters on the brink of collapse for a trio of reasons— a wife might find trivial excuses to return to her maika, a husband may wander because he lacks paternal duties, and there's always an individual present to whisper in the husband's ear about the dire need for an heir through second marriage.

But here's what I think: while children might make a couple think twice before splitting, they are not saviors sent to rescue a failing marriage. The harsh truth is that men might still stray and women might still walk away. And here's the real kicker—if children are born into a union just to patch up cracks, we're not really saving the marriage; we're burdening these young lives with an inheritance of unresolved trauma.

Bringing a child into the world with the hope they will glue a fragile relationship back together is a gamble with high stakes. The issues that troubled the marriage pre-parenthood won't magically disappear postpartum. Instead, they often deepen, compounded by the sleepless nights and relentless demands of new parenthood. In reality, having a baby is not and should never be seen as a tool to mend a faltering relationship. It's a lifelong commitment, not a marriage band-aid.

Right from the start, Arooj had a nagging feeling that her marriage to Badar was like trying to mix oil and water. Love was there, no doubt, but their differences were too deep, too stark. Every discussion ended in a deadlock, every decision was a battlefield. You often hear people say that opposites attract, but Arooj could tell you that in their case, it was more like "opposites attack." *Research and psychologists back this up too, suggesting that opposites might make for a great movie plot, but in real life, they rarely mesh well.*

Living with someone who sees the world through an entirely different lens doesn't just complicate things—it can make you feel like you're constantly at war in your own home. Both Arooj and Badar frequently found themselves wondering if they were meant to be with someone else, someone whose rhythm matched their own. This wasn't just about occasional disagreements; it was a daily struggle, leaving them both to ponder if perhaps their paths were meant to diverge, finding harmony with others whose life tunes resonated more closely with their own.

Arooj didn't need anyone to suggest having a child as a solution to her and Badar's relentless disagreements. She came to the conclusion on her own, harboring a hope that is common yet often misguided. She thought that if she and Badar could barely agree on anything from dawn till dusk, maybe, just maybe, they would find common ground in their love for a child. The emotional divides—him with his heart on his sleeve and her with her calculated logic—seemed bridgeable through the shared responsibility and love for a child. Arooj felt that they'd get better if only *they were complete.* She imagined a middle ground, a tiny oasis of peace, where they could meet away from their daily conflicts. It was an act of hope, an effort to forge a bond strong enough to overcome their differences.

To Arooj's surprise and initial relief, the arrival of their baby seemed to cast a temporary spell of peace over their turbulent marriage. During her pregnancy, there was a noticeable shift in their dynamic. Badar's gaze softened, shedding the usual bitterness for something tender, reminiscent of the love that had first drawn them together. They found themselves reconnecting, venturing out on dates, and enjoying each other's company in a way that had seemed lost to the past.

However, this period of harmony was fleeting. While the baby brought moments of joy and a brief respite from their struggles, it didn't resolve the deep-seated issues that plagued their relationship. The underlying conflicts, the fundamental differences in how they viewed the world—it all remained, simmering beneath the surface. They were better, yes, but far from healed. The presence of their child acted as a bandage, covering but not curing the wounds that continued to divide them.

Arooj had always understood, deep down, that children aren't magical cures for fractured relationships. They aren't tools or salves to patch up the gaping holes in a troubled marriage. She knew that while children might enrich and add joy to a union, they aren't meant to be the foundation upon which a marriage is built or repaired. Yet, despite this knowledge, Arooj clung to a sliver of hope that their situation might be the exception—that somehow, their little one could bring them together in a lasting way.

Then one very regular afternoon, when the curry was in the pot, and the dispenser needed to be turned on, and the massi was requesting a leave because her brother had died for the third time, something in Arooj snapped. The weight of her unfulfilled marriage, the relentless hope that somehow, a child could mend the irreparable, had finally become too much to bear. She felt something deep within her fracture. In that moment, she knew: that not even their son could salvage what had long been broken between her and Badar.

As she stood there, resolved to walk away, Badar began to confess. His words tumbled out in a rush, admitting that he too was exhausted from pretending. He offered her stability, a life of comfort for her and their child if she chose to stay, but Arooj knew that mere provision was no substitute for genuine happiness.

They both deserved more than coexistence; they deserved joy, fulfillment, and love—real love, not just the remnants of a bond held together by obligation and appearances.

Moved by their mutual acknowledgment of their situation, and for the sake of their son, they decided to try therapy. It was transformative in ways neither expected. Therapy didn't repair their marriage, but it did make them better individuals—more present, more understanding parents. Their relationship with their son deepened, fortified by their joint commitment to his well-being rather than a strained partnership.

Seven years into their marriage, with grace and mutual respect, Arooj and Badar decided to part ways. They eventually found love again with others, people with whom they could share the kind of happiness they had once hoped to find with each other.

However, there is also the case of Munawar Aunty's daughter Zari, whose relationship with her husband started on fairly rough grounds because she had a falling out with her mother-in-law and her entire day was full of complaining about his mother to her husband. There were problems with the house favourite *dewrani*, with the maid who was a tell-tale, and with all the other people that her MIL had supposedly turned against her new *bahu*. Over here, in all honesty, was the mistake of both women; the *saas* and the *bahu*. Zari and her mother-in-law were both strong-willed women, brimming with pride and marred by a massive communication gap that festered through thirty days packed with misunderstandings and household politics. The tension spilled over, deeply straining Zari's relationship with her husband to a breaking point, leading both families to consider that perhaps a separation would be the kindest solution.

However, just as they were about to part ways, Zari

discovered she was pregnant. This unexpected twist prompted her to keep the baby, and her husband, Hamid, to delay their mutual decision to divorce. In an unforeseen turn of events, the crisis that seemed destined to split them apart became the crisis that held them together. The divorce that seemed inevitable never came to pass.

Now, two decades later, Zari and Hamid are still together, parents to a nineteen-year-old daughter and a ten-year-old son. In their case, the arrival of their first child created a new context for their relationship—one where they found reasons to rebuild rather than dismantle. This isn't to say that children are a cure-all for marital issues, but in Zari and Hamid's case, becoming parents gave them a new lens through which to see each other and their relationship, helping them steer through their challenges and solidify a bond that has endured for over twenty years. Sometimes, indeed, a child does make a difference. Still, it's crucial to note that while Zari and Hamid's story turned out positively, planning a child purely as a strategy to save a troubled marriage is far from advisable. Children can indeed bring couples closer together, offering new perspectives and shared responsibilities that can strengthen a bond. However, relying on a child to bridge deep, unresolved marital issues places an unfair burden on the child and doesn't address the underlying problems that are causing the discord.

Babies are not a remedy for marital strife. They are individuals who will grow up with needs and emotions of their own. Bringing a child into a relationship in crisis can complicate matters further, adding layers of stress and responsibility to an already fragile union. Effective communication, counseling, and mutual understanding are essential tools for repairing relationships, not the added pressure of parenthood.

For couples facing difficulties, it's important to first explore these avenues and find solid ground in their relationship. If a couple can heal their rifts and choose to start a family from a place of love and stability, then a child can be a beautiful addition to their life together—not the glue designed to hold a breaking relationship together.

———

Dear Ayesha,

In ancient Rome, women of nobility would invoke Juno, the goddess of marriage, to bless their unions and dispel strife. They believed that divine intervention could sweep away marital discord like chaff in the wind. Across the seas in Japan, the revered onna-bugeisha, female samurai, would often use their diplomatic prowess to forge alliances and heal rifts within their clans, proving that sometimes, the pen—or the carefully spoken word—could be mightier than the sword.

Similarly, in the far reaches of the Punjab, women would resort to the ancient practice of desi jharu, literally sweeping away the negativity that threatened their domestic bliss with brooms crafted from sacred grass.

The wisdom here, dear Ayesha, is poignant: sometimes, the bedbugs must indeed be treated—whether by throwing out old mattresses or by burning the linens that harbor these stubborn pests. The allegory for our modern lives couldn't be clearer. Some conflicts within a marriage can be resolved with time and effort, much like washing away the stains on well-loved sheets. Yet, other times, these disruptions are so deep-seated that they require more drastic measures—perhaps an entire renewal of the household, or even stepping away from what cannot be salvaged.

Let these ancient narratives remind us that while our battles may not be with literal insects, the essence of conflict remains the same. And just as our ancestors knew, not every bug is worth the bite; sometimes, the bravest thing we can do is decide when to mend and when to move on, ensuring our personal peace isn't compromised.

Love, the jinns.

Chapter 7

The One That Got Away

In every life story, there's often a chapter dedicated to the one that got away—the person who slipped through our fingers like sand, leaving behind nothing but a soft echo of what might have been. It's a tale as old as time, wrapped in the sweet sorrow of missed connections and lingering what-ifs. Aik purani yaad that tugs at the heartstrings.

If your heart still harbors a flicker for a lost love, know that you walk a path lined with the echoes of many who have come before you. But here's the crux: dwelling on a lost love isn't just about nursing an old wound—it's about understanding what these feelings represent.

For those of you torn between the chapters of a past romance and your present, consider this: living in the shadows of what was is an injustice to what is. Reflect on your lost love not as the missing piece of your zindagi, but as a guidepost that helped shape your understanding of love and desire.

And when you do find the one who stays, let the past not overshadow but illuminate the love you can give and receive.

Because, in the end, they're only the one who got away until you meet the one who makes you understand why it never worked out with anyone else.

Handling the emotional aftermath of a relationship isn't bound by any timetable, nor is it confined to a specific set of emotions. It's alright to wade through a mix of sadness, frustration, or even a lingering hope—each feeling carving its own path toward healing. Embrace these waves; let them wash over you, and in their wake, you'll find clarity and the strength to move forward. But remember, once you've welcomed someone new into your life, resist the urge to measure them against a past love. They are not a replacement but a new beginning—a reason unveiled why the past didn't unfold as you once wished.

It's often not the person themselves you're mourning, but the dazzling future you'd painted together. Don't let yourself circle endlessly in the whys and what-ifs of it all. Truth is, if that relationship was as perfect as your daydreams, it wouldn't be in the past.

And remember, holding on to bitterness is like holding onto a hot coal, hoping the other person feels the burn. What happened to Alina was not fair, for she had loved her fiancé more than she had ever loved a man but when he called it off, Alina started on a crusade to speak ill of him whilst he didn't speak of her at all. It's not about painting everything with rose-tinted glasses; it's about choosing not to dwell in a shadowy past. Letting go of resentment frees you more than it frees them! It opens up space in your life for genuine joy and peace, allowing you to embrace the love and opportunities that are right in front of you. Release the past not because it wasn't significant, but because you deserve the serenity that comes with moving forward.

Sometimes, it feels like you've lost part of yourself when they leave. It's like dropping your morning chai cup—it shatters, and you're left trying to pick up the pieces, thinking if you can just find all of them, maybe you can put it back together. But here's the thing: sometimes, it's not about piecing back the old but about finding the courage to start anew. The chai will still taste the same.

Accepting that a part of your old life is over isn't just a tough pill to swallow; it's a bitter one. But it's also the pill that starts the healing. It's realizing that even without that part of you, you can still be whole, maybe even more whole than before. You're not just rebuilding—you're redefining. It's about saying *Allah Hafiz* to who you were with them and *Salam* to who you can become without them. This isn't just moving on; it's moving up.

Often, relationships crumble not just because of conflict, but from a deep-seated lack of understanding about our own needs. By gaining clarity about who you are and what you truly need, you empower yourself and your partner. This self-awareness will allow your current or future partner to better fulfill their role in the relationship, fostering a deeper, more meaningful connection.

And so know this: Relationships don't always end because two people *did something wrong* to each other—they end because two people are sometimes *wrong for* each other.

Batool Aunty, a family friend who often popped by our bustling joint family setup, had a knack for weaving poetic thoughts about life's what-ifs. Despite a pretty good marriage with Yawar Khan, where she had perks like a fancy car and kids in top-notch schools, her mind occasionally drifted to a parallel universe where she married her cousin Rizwan instead. She'd imagine a life back in Karachi, closer to the family, with kids sporting the cute, button-like eyes typical of her family line. But then reality would pull her back—sure, her kids with Yawar had noses a bit too prominent, yet they also had a dad who adored them and provided a life many dreamed of.

Sometimes, she'd mull over these thoughts aloud. Maybe part of her wrestled with the idea of living that other life, but deep down, Batool Aunty knew comparing the two was like trying to blend oil and water. It's a bit unfair, really—fantasizing about a life you never lived while the one you're living has its own sweet perks. It's a gentle reminder: the grass might look greener on the other side, but it still needs watering. Embrace where you're planted. After all, life isn't about finding the perfect scenario but making the most of the one you're in.

In a modern saga spun out across the digital landscape, an old acquaintance found her love life unwittingly under the social media spotlight. Dreaming of forever, she and her fiancé had become local celebrities on social media. But life, as it does, had other plans. Out of nowhere, he broke off their engagement and married someone else they both knew. The betrayal was public, the heartbreak palpable. The healing began when someone new entered her life, someone who had followed her story and understood the depth of her pain. This understanding allowed him to approach her with patience and grace. And they did a remarkable thing; together, they retraced her favorite spots on MM Alam Road, to replace her old memories. Now, if you scroll through her feed, you see a woman transformed by resilience. Her smile, brighter than before, speaks to a simple truth: sometimes, the detours life throws at us, painful as they may be, lead us to where we're meant to be. God's plans, mysterious and more meaningful than we often understand, always have a way of guiding us home—reminding us that He cares, infinitely more than we can comprehend.

But with that, arises the question of what happens to those with an ill fate? Indeed, the realm of marriage, much like any deep commitment, carries its share of risks and rewards—a true gamble of hearts and hopes. Consider the ones who, propelled by love and hope, find themselves tethered to souls who neither understand nor cherish them. It's a harsh reality for some, who enter marriage with dreams of companionship, only to find themselves ensnared in a union marked by indifference or, worse, disdain for their past affections! I see *amis* going around saying that they'll accept the first suitable proposal that knocks on their door because they trust God. Yes, one needs to have *tawakul*, but you do not leave your wedding gold lying around, believing that God will protect it. You lock it up in a safe with a code and then leave it up to God to safeguard it. You cannot leave your *jahez ki car,* (which should have stayed with your father in the first place), unlocked in the bustling Liberty market, and then look at the sky, asking God to protect the vehicle your man seldom lets you drive. You leave it locked and parked in a safe spot because God has given you the brain to do so. Hence, *shaadi* is no different. Similarly, the process of choosing a spouse, especially for one's daughter, should be a meticulous one: engage with the family, vet their backgrounds, align their values and lifestyles with yours, and only then, once due diligence is done, should you lean on your faith. To dismiss glaring red flags with the hope that a wife will later mold her husband into the man he ought to be is not just folly. Your daughter will then forever be hung up on the one who got away.

Marriage, in its essence, should be a covenant entered into with both eyes open, where the risks are known and the safeguards are set. Only then, once everything humanly possible has been done, does one leave the rest to fate, embracing whatever comes as part of the divine plan. True *tawakul*, or trust in God, operates not in the absence of action but alongside earnest effort.

I've also witnessed women married to commendable men who may not resemble the dashing figures from their pasts. And yet, they find themselves unjustly critiquing their husband's receding hairline, the unique curve of his nose, or his less-than-towering stature. Imagine, for a moment, if these devoted husbands began to retaliate by lamenting over their wives' softer bellies, the occasional chin hair, or the lingering scent of *khichdi* that perfumes their day.

Physical attraction, indeed, holds its sway, and no one is suggesting that men roam about with unkempt bellies and the aroma of cigars. However, the immutable features with which one is born should hardly be fodder for fault-finding. Remember, you chose this man as your partner. It's worth considering that after birthing two children, your own bloom may fade a bit faster than your husband's—women often show their years sooner, and the mirror will reflect these changes as the seasons pass and you wouldn't want any comments on that.

Never overlook a man who cherishes you, who offers respect, and defends your corner for he is worth more than a handsome face that promised the moon yet fled at the first sign of maternal disapproval: *Ami nahin maan rahein*. In the end, the true measure of a partner lies not in the superficialities of appearance but in the strength of their character and the depth of their devotion.

———

Dear Ayesha,

Perhaps the one who left had a voice sweeter than the syrupy ooze of a chum chum, never once cloying, always just right. Perhaps he had the charisma that lit up the room, a smile that sparked wild dreams, and a touch that felt like summer rain on parched earth. And yes, maybe he had that broad chest and a smile that set your heart aflutter, his touch igniting sparks. Yet here you are, beside another whose build might not stir tales of epic romances, whose mustache you claim tickles more than it tempts, giving you more rashes than rushes. Here beside you now is someone whose laughter doesn't echo quite as loudly, whose touch is more familiar than thrilling. His features may not sketch the archetypal hero of your youthful fantasies but in his presence, there's a genuine peace, a sense of belonging that no thrilling storm could offer. This quiet companionship, like still water, nurtures and sustains you through every season of life. Juice you can't, but water you can have every day.

Love, the jinns.

Chapter 8

The Rocky Rishta

Not all men have the tendency to cheat but those who do might or might not have a reason for doing so. Now, none of the following reasons justify why Ali disappeared at dawn for milk and hasn't yet found his way back, but, they do give insight on why, in general, men can be unfaithful.

Sometimes, a man is done with having *daal* everyday, not knowing that the specific plate of lentils is what keeps him that fit and he has forgotten that since childhood it was his favorite comfort meal. The man is done and wants a way out. He's looking for change, not because he needs it, but because he's forgotten the value of what he has at home. This type of cheating is often remorseless, at least until reality strikes back. Instead of facing tough conversations, he finds it easier to cheat, sidestepping the issues at home in search of something new.

Sometimes, the act of cheating stems from deeper, more unsettling personality traits. Men who betray their partners might be sociopaths, narcissists, or simply individuals who care very little about the feelings of others. For these men, the pursuit of another relationship is straightforward and unburdened by guilt—it's simply about wanting someone else. There's no complex puzzle to solve with this kind of cheater. Even before the cheating, their behavioral traits are enough evidence to understand that you've unfortunately married expired *mithae*.

Sometimes, infidelity is driven by a raw, unsettling desire for revenge. It may seem far-fetched, but some men cheat not out of lust but anger. The woman in their lives might not have strayed herself, but perhaps she's triggered a deep-seated rage that prompts these men to seek retribution in the most hurtful way they know. Picture this: as children, these are the type who might have spitefully dipped their sibling's toothbrush in toilet water. For these types of men, *badla* is important. Studies suggest these revenge-driven cheaters sometimes keep their actions secret to savor the silent victory; other times, they make sure their partner finds out, twisting the knife to maximize the pain.

Then there's the matter of substance abuse. Men like Akbar or Ali, who might otherwise be charming and loving husbands, find their resolve crumbling under the influence. Alcohol or drugs can hijack their better judgment, leading them down paths they might never consider sober. Chances are that he'll go down that road again. Because to him, *the bottle made me do it, jaan. You know it wasn't me.*

Then there's the tangled web of mental anguish—some men, caught in the grips of stress or depression, wrongly believe that an affair might lighten their burdens. While therapy might be a far more appropriate choice, these men choose infidelity as a misguided form of self-medication. When we women face the blues, we stuff three *aloo parhattas* followed by desi Chinese down our throats, not betrayal. So, while mental challenges are real and tough, using them as a crutch to justify infidelity hardly seems fair or justifiable.

On the flip side, there are men ensnared in relationships with women who might not appreciate them—the Fatimas who inadvertently push their men away with their coldness or neglect. It's a harsh cycle, one where these men, starved for approval and warmth, end up in the arms of another woman. Men too can be stuck in a vicious toxic cycle and since they don't get appreciation from the one person they look up to the most, they seek validation elsewhere. Unlike the reckless abandon in other scenarios, this type of infidelity often stems from a strong sense of neglect and a craving for connection. This doesn't make the act any less damaging, but unlike other forms of cheating, this scenario often holds a glimmer of hope for reconciliation and healing, provided both partners are willing to acknowledge their faults and work towards mending the rift.

Diving into a somewhat overlooked chapter from the past, here's a truth you wouldn't find in those 90's marriage help books—a topic they considered too taboo: Some men far away from the real understanding of religion, are queer and they are not given the help that they need. Instead of fixing them, their *amis* marry them off. This misguided attempt unwittingly drags their wives into complex emotional turmoil.

Hassan's tale is a classic example of how complex relationships can be. He's the kind of man who admits to being used to his wife, describing his feelings as mere attachment, but confesses he has never been truly in love with her. This confession reflects a common dilemma: individuals like Hassan remain in relationships out of habit or duty while secretly yearning for the thrilling sensation of falling in love. These feelings often lead them to seek excitement outside their marriage, perhaps with a colleague or a casual acquaintance. And then, *they blame their cheating on having truly loved.*

Mohid, despite owning two plazas and three showrooms,

has the emotional depth of a teenage boy. He's a man who can run a business but can't handle his own emotions without causing a storm at home. He needs to be spanked by his *aba jee* during the day and needs to be sent to a therapist in the evening to regulate his emotions so he doesn't traumatize his poor wife. His wife, caught in the whirlwind of his teenage-like tantrums, might find some peace if Mohid learned to manage his heart as well as he manages his assets.

Now that we've peeled back the layers on why some men stray, let's pivot to the real crux of the matter: what to do if you find out your partner has cheated.

When the unthinkable happens and you discover that Azeem, the man you trusted, has stepped out on the relationship, it's like a storm has swept through your life, uprooting everything that felt stable. The flood of emotions—shock, anger, sorrow, and disbelief—is overwhelming.

First things first: take a breath. Accepting that it happened doesn't mean you condone it, but it's the first step in dealing with the chaos. Revenge might seem tempting in your fiery state; you might fantasize about unleashing your fury on social media or evening the score by stepping out yourself. But pause and think—these impulses, while intensely satisfying at the moment, often fan the flames of your anger, holding you back from true healing.

If you're contemplating giving this relationship another shot, remember that retaliatory actions can poison any prospects of reconciliation. On the flip side, if you're leaning towards walking away, is the drama of revenge truly worth your energy? Revenge is a dish that, no matter how spicy and satisfying, often leaves a bitter aftertaste.

And when it comes to confiding in your family or friends, tread carefully. Their instinct to protect you will kick in, sparking a chorus of "leave him!" But remember, they aren't privy to the full complexity of your relationship. This journey, fraught with decisions about staying, leaving, forgiving, or forgetting, is yours to handle. For now, keep the circle of trust tight and the details close to your heart. Your healing needs space, away from the prying eyes and well-meaning but often overwhelming opinions of others.

Steering through the aftermath of betrayal is akin to riding the roughest waves of a storm. It's more than just emotional upheaval; your body might react too. You could find yourself battling nausea or insomnia, your appetite might vanish, or you could end up overeating in search of comfort. There might be days during the brightest summers when you find yourself shivering, clutching a blanket around your shaking body as if the chill of betrayal has seeped into your bones.

Yet, here's the thing—you won't perish in this storm. The world hasn't ended. These turbulent feelings will pass. It's essential now, more than ever, to care gently for yourself. Keep nourishing meals on your plate, set a regular sleep schedule, and find moments for movement each day. Stay hydrated. It's not merely about enduring but rebuilding yourself, finding peace in routine, and drawing strength from the simple, daily acts of self-care. This isn't just survival; it's about emerging resilient, finding joy again on your own terms, and learning to prioritize your well-being above all.

Draw a firm line when it comes to involving the kids. Their hearts are tender; their roles, simple—just to be your children, not your confidants in marital strife. If you're managing the choppy waters of a relationship shaken by infidelity, remember to keep your children safely ashore. Sharing the burdensome details of an affair can place an unfair weight on their shoulders, creating unnecessary stress and forcing them into a no-win situation of side-taking. Protect their innocence and their peace; let them remain blissfully unaware of the adult complexities that lie beyond their emotional reach. That little brain shouldn't have to know that his hero *papa* slept with *Aunty* Shameem, the mother of his best friend, who he shares his lunch-time nuggets with.

Involve the *khandaan* afterwards. Before bringing the whole clan into the mix, it's wise to first sit down with a couple's counselor. Think of it as doing a bit of recon before you bring in the big guns. This isn't just any squabble—it's a full-blown marital crisis, and you don't want to go into that battle unprepared. A good counselor acts like your personal guide through this emotional minefield, helping you to understand the whys and hows, and keeping the communication lines open without things blowing up. You'll have the chance to sort through your feelings and your partner's actions with someone who's trained to manage such messes. This way, if it comes to calling it quits, you'll know you've given it your all, making your decision from a place of calm and clarity, not just hurt and haste.

If you're grappling with the aftermath of an affair, it's a pivotal moment to consider not just your emotional landscape, but the practicalities as well. Where will you live? Do you have the financial cushion necessary to cover your essentials? If children are part of the equation, what kind of custody arrangement would be best?

It's a whirlwind, no doubt, and not one to face alone. Lean on your loved ones for support as you handle these murky waters. Consider all your options. Take Samina *apa*, for instance. She knew her husband's flaws—his departures and returns like clockwork. She knew that her husband had a pattern, and that at the end of the episode he returned home to her, and so she made the difficult decision to stay in the marriage for all the things he did that made her smile, and not for one thing where he broke her heart. She made this decision due to the lifestyle that she had gotten used to and the future of the children. The four cars, the Oasis membership, the two *nands* who tried to make their brother understand and showered Samina *apa* and her daughters with gifts, and the expensive schools that took fees in dollars - Samina *apa* chose to stay for the comfort. On the flip side, there's Rabiya Kalsoom, a tough cookie I worked with on Davis Road—a place as chaotic as her personal life turned out to be. She made the painful but clear decision to leave, knowing that the trust was irreparably broken. She knew that her *bhabhi* was a handful and that her *bhai* tried his level best to make her stay in that marriage but deep down, Rabiya understood that she could never be the same with her husband.

Dealing with an affair forces a crossroads—one that doesn't always have to lead to the end of your marriage. It's about taking stock of what remains, what's broken, and what can be rebuilt. With time, whether you choose to rebuild together or apart, clarity comes, guiding you towards the next chapter of your life.

A friend who insisted we try the new crepes in DHA Phase 6, turned to me with a worry crinkling her brow. She wanted to know how one could tell if their partner was unfaithful. I told her that *women just know.* Even if they've not caught him yet, deep down they are well aware of what their man is capable of. From being emotionally disconnected, to showing significant changes in their behavior, to getting less excited by you...the list of suspicions is endless. She kept chewing on her bite, her eyes wide open. She then nodded, her fork pausing mid-air as she mulled over signs like emotional distance, abrupt behavioral changes, and a waning enthusiasm—all of which she sadly recognized in her husband. But then again, this was the same friend who just six months ago, went through a lot of ordeal to prove that her *nand* gifted her a fake Gucci, only to find out that it was real and she also feigned fainting to avoid going to an in-laws' funeral because her upper-lip and chin weren't lasered. I'm not saying her husband is a saint, but jumping to conclusions about infidelity based on past suspicions might not be fair. This friend tends to dramatize, and although it's entirely possible her husband might stray, it seems unlikely at the moment, given what I know of him. Contrastingly, another friend from our circle wasn't so fortunate; her husband did stray, and she's the first to back any of our friend's suspicions, even suggesting spy apps for peace of mind. This kind of vigilance can complicate relationships. Don't get me wrong - I believe that *if you share a bed, you can definitely share phone passwords* but —letting suspicions dictate your life can lead to unnecessary turmoil. Trust is delicate, and without it, even the strongest bonds can fray.

There will often be times when you or your husband will be tempted to cheat, but knowing where the boundaries lie and having clear, open communication about expectations can safeguard your relationship against such heartbreak. Yet, in the tangled web of life, not all suspicions lead to truths, and not all doubts are unfounded. It's crucial to approach such delicate situations with a balanced perspective, not letting jealousy cloud judgment or naivety blind you to red flags.

If you choose to stay, let it stem from a place of true hope in the power of forgiveness and the chance for a fresh start, not merely out of fear of the unknown or the daunting prospect of a single life. On the flip side, if you feel the need to walk away, do it with your head held high, knowing you're not just fleeing a broken relationship, but moving towards a future where joy and respect wait on the horizon.

Remember, choosing to leave isn't giving up on love; it's

asserting that you deserve a love that's full and free from shadows. Every ending carves out the space for a new beginning—maybe, just maybe, this is your first step toward finding a relationship that truly lifts you up and lights your path forward.

———

Dear Ayesha,

Farhan is a loving man. His eyes light up six years after marriage - the same way they did when he realized that he was in love with you. It wasn't love at first sight, in fact, you two were in the same room but did not notice each other. If in life, there ever comes a time, God forbid, that you two sit in a room and act as strangers like you once were, knowing that there isn't anything left to cling on to, understand that it will be difficult to live without a person who you synced your breaths to, whose scent made you feel alive and on most days after he's gone, you'll almost drown in a pool of water that doesn't even cover your legs. Up and down. Up and down. In the waves. You'll almost sleep in three days. You'll almost taste the aloo ghosht that has suddenly lost flavor and one fine day the sleep and the flavor will return and you won't drown in the pool meant for children. You'll live.

Don't be scared if this ever happens. Because if he chooses to love and if he chooses to stay, one day he will still leave the bed for the grave. And then you'll lose him to not another woman, but God. So don't be scared, when this happens.

Love, the jinns.

Chapter 9

Massi Musibatein

They say before we were born into this world, we existed among spirits in a realm beyond. It's there we formed connections or aversions that echo in our present lives. Imagine that! The souls we felt drawn to there are the ones we vibe with instantly here on earth, and those we recoiled from? Well, they're the ones we just can't seem to gel with, no matter how hard we try. I'm not talking about evil, good-for-nothing, *rishta*-sabotaging individuals. Sure, they exist too but there are also people so drastically different than you, that you cannot understand them and they cannot understand you. This chapter dives into the perplexing relationships with people we meet through marriage—like a *saas* who's from another planet of perspective, or a *nand*'s teenage daughter who's a constant, enigmatic presence in your home.

Now, these people can make life difficult, in many ways, knowingly and unknowingly. These are the folks who can make our days a bit more challenging, in both big and small ways. Yet, no matter the urge, distancing ourselves isn't an option. Bound by the chains of social and familial norms, these relationships demand navigation—a play of diplomacy on a stage not of our choosing. We call these intriguing yet baffling beings *massi musibatein (mm)* —the necessary nuisances of our lives.

In my circle, there's no shortage of folks wrestling with their very own *massi musibatein*. There's one relative in particular—whose name I'll keep under wraps—but her FIL is a chapter unto himself. You see, a few years back, he had quite the tumble off a bridge in Murree, and though he emerged with a seemingly intact body, his mind began to march to a different drum. Medical tests showed nothing amiss, and his devotion to prayers remained impeccable, yet his daily doings stray far from the path of the wise. In fact, he does the silliest of things and then the most embarrassing ones too and then blames it on his fall. This man turns household norms into a circus; he'll snatch his young granddaughter's lunch right from under her nose, hissing if she dared complain, despite having wolfed down his own meal. Not stopping there, he'll spill water only to slip in it, creating scenes that leave him weeping amidst the chaos. The family is super well off, so the FIL need not work, but whatever he does at home, certainly does not work for the others. Imagine a man, lost in his own world, treating life like a video game—tossing about chaos with the misguided belief that a simple reset could mend all. The latest from this domestic front was his baffling decision to donate every single pair of his wife's shoes to passersby. The one pair that was left was found behind the toilet seat of a locked room. This *mm* parades as a prosperous retired businessman, a jovial father of five who chortles at his own burps! A figure of stability and jest, possessing everything yet governing a realm of unpredictability under his own roof.

Then, there's an unmarried friend whose sister's husband spends half the week at their place. He's great with handling their now partially blind *abu's* finances, and truth be told he helps around the house when needed too. *But*, this man, who doubles as a household drill sergeant, has taken it upon himself to monitor my friend's every move. Since that friend has been rejected due to being overweight by potential suitors, the sister's husband will drop by at Fajr, wake up by the friend and have her jog, then he'll weigh her each day and police her diet like a hawk. If the friend dares to sneak an extra *samosa*, there he is, swiping the plate away as if calories were contraband. It doesn't end with food; he's got the audacity to check her phone, vet her calls, and dictate her daily routines. He has a say in all her matters. *All of them.* The married sister can't set boundaries, the *ami jee* is too smitten by the *damad* because he once arranged a blood donation for her, and the *abu* is as quiet as a mouse. Furthermore, the married sister has been given a second chance due to her online cheating on a book forum with an alleged Korean man - which further complicates things. And thus, nothing can be done to tame this *mm*.

It's a classic case of a well-meaning family member turning into a *massi musibatein*, believing he's steering the ship when in fact, he's rocking the boat for everyone onboard.

Here's an interesting tale: a second cousin of mine is married into a well-off family whose loyal kitchen *massi* since fourteen years is an *mm*. Let's call the cousin Saima and the *massi* Jamila. Now, this *massi* Jamila took an instant dislike to Saima. From the get-go, there was friction, and it wasn't just the occasional clash over cupboard spaces; it was about everything, down to how to properly season a biryani.

One fateful day, Saima, trying to assert some control in her new kitchen, corrected *massi* Jamila on a dish. Not just a verbal suggestion—oh no, Saima had *massi* Jamila stand beside her while she demonstrated the 'right' way to do it. *Massi* Jamila complied, but tears streamed down her cheeks, hurt by the thought: *Kal ki bachi mujhe sikhae gi?*

Saima, feeling a tad guilty, apologized, but the damage was done. She shared the tale with her mother-in-law, thinking it was a minor kitchen scuffle. But when she returned from a family wedding in her father's village, she walked back into a war zone. *Massi* Jamila had morphed into a formidable foe, determined to make every waking moment a challenge for Saima, sniping at her for every perceived slight, turning every misstep into a catastrophe. And the icing on this chaotic cake? Saima's husband, a gem in most respects, had his blinders on. *Massi humari ma ki jaisi hain*, he'd say, placing *massi* on a pedestal, leaving Saima to handle the stormy waters of domestic politics with this *mm* alone. A tale of kitchen wars, wounded pride, and the delicate balance of new family dynamics, where not even the sweetest gulab jamun can smooth over the bitterness brewing in the background.

All *mms*—share a few troubling traits, woven into their very essence like a stubborn stain on a favorite shalwar kameez. First off, they're resistant to change; engaging with them is akin to having a heart-to-heart with a brick wall. Immovable and impassive, they seem to have set their ways in concrete.

These *mms* don't just dodge responsibility for their actions; they often act as though your mere existence is the pebble in their shoe, irritating and unavoidable. Don't expect them to make an effort to get along or smooth over tensions; they've hung up their gloves long ago.

Curiously, these perplexing personalities usually have a solid rapport with other family members, making any attempt by you to cast them in a less favorable light backfire spectacularly. You end up looking like the villain in a drama where everyone else is blissfully unaware of the antagonist's plot.

Communication with an *mm* is a complicated challenge. They might talk over you as if your words weigh less than air, or give you the cold shoulder, dismissing your thoughts before they've even fully formed. Some are masters of the passive-aggressive jab, wrapping cruelty in a veneer of politeness that leaves you second-guessing the intent behind their words.

Breakfast for the *mm* is a bowl of criticism cereal, sprinkled with a hefty dose of disdain. These folks can shoot down ideas and dreams faster than a seasoned sharpshooter, leaving nothing and no one up to their standards. And if you're the unfortunate soul closest to them, brace yourself—their barbs aren't just sharp; they're personal.

In their world, empathy is as scarce as a sincere compliment. They have a retort ready for every situation, armed with a baffling lack of sensitivity when it comes to your feelings. Engaging with an *mm* often leaves you drained, doubting, and dismayed, wondering if there's ever a way to turn this fraught relationship into a peaceful coexistence.

Now that we've untangled exactly what an *mm* is—and I'm willing to bet we've all crossed paths with one at some point— it's crucial to discuss how to live alongside them without jeopardizing our sanity.

Our *amis* often counsel us to just "smile and bear it." *Sabr,* they preach, and plenty of it. But what they sometimes miss is that dealing with a truly difficult person isn't just about enduring their presence. These encounters can stick to your thoughts like unwelcome gum on a shoe, pestering you long after the moment has passed.

Continually stuffing down those troublesome interactions isn't just exhausting; it's like slowly sipping poison. Day by day, month by month, year by year, the toxicity builds up, seeping into your well-being until you find your mental health fraying at the edges. So, *while sabr is golden, preserving your inner peace is priceless.* How do we manage this delicate balance? That's the puzzle we need to piece together.

Managing the stormy waters with your *mm* starts with a bit of detective work: figuring out what drew their sights to you. It might be something you did, knowingly or unknowingly, that made you their mark, or perhaps it's simply because you've been too passive, making you an easy target. Understanding the root of their focus isn't about assigning blame to yourself; rather, it's about shedding light on the situation to better handle it. It's important to remember that most *mms* don't wake up with a plan to make your day harder; their actions are often spurred by their own unresolved issues or insecurities that you just happen to trigger.

The second step is to pay attention to how you react. It is crucial to turn the lens inward and assess your reactions. How do you feel when faced with their antics? Frustrated, demeaned, or perhaps invisible? Identifying your emotions helps you step back from the immediacy of the situation and approach it with a cooler head. Recognize this: *mms* are adept at sensing weakness or disturbance—they feed off your emotional responses. By managing your reactions, you rob them of their power. They often manipulate these reactions to paint you as the unstable one, using your justifiable upset to rally others to their side. Understanding and controlling your response is key to disarming their influence and keeping your peace.

Step three is about stepping into their world, even if just for a moment. Take a deep dive into understanding your *mm's* viewpoint: if you were in their shoes, with their history and their burdens, how might you perceive the world? This exercise isn't about justifying their behavior but about uncovering the reasons behind it. It's about empathy—seeing through their eyes might reveal why they act the way they do.

Understanding their perspective can be enlightening. For instance, Zainab was forbidden to visit her parents more than once in six months by her otherwise caring mother-in-law because all her life she wasn't permitted to visit *her* folks. She could have done the exact opposite with her daughter-in-law, knowing how she felt, but she chose not to. From Zainab's mother-in-law's point of view, this was a generous allowance, a significant easing of the rules she herself had lived under. Eventually, two years after marriage, Zainab got her way but the key point that helped her here and in most other aspects was the very fact that her MIL's MIL was not a great MIL and so *Zainab's MIL* had a lot of toxic unlearning to do.

Recognizing this helped Zainab steer her relationship with more grace and patience. Over time, she managed to gently shift her mother-in-law's stance by demonstrating understanding and gradually introducing her to a new way of thinking. This approach not only improved their relationship but also allowed Zainab more freedom, illustrating how empathy can pave the way for change. By putting yourself in their position, you're not excusing their behavior but rather opening the door to more compassionate and effective communication.

Step four in handling your *mm* revolves around communication, but it must be approached with care. Imagine planning your talk like setting the stage for a delicate performance. You wouldn't rush the opening scene; similarly, you should pick a quiet moment for this conversation, preferably in a private setting to avoid public fallout. If your *mm* has a habit of throwing things out of proportion and there is a risk of a misunderstanding, having someone else there can help keep things clear and on track.

Think about what you want to say in advance. Keeping the

discussion focused can prevent it from derailing and turning into an emotional battlefield. For instance, if your *mm* has a knack for diverting discussions to unrelated issues, it's like her bringing up every forgotten birthday or minor slight just as you're addressing something critical. By preparing your points, you remain the director of this conversation.

However, know when to pause. If tensions rise, propose a timeout with the intention to revisit the discussion later. This isn't surrender—it's tactical withdrawal. My chacha's *mm* was his step father-in-law who had tricky moods. Chacha found that short, frequent talks on neutral grounds, like during a walk in the park with the *mm* who loved to brisk walk after the evening meal helped more than confronting the *mm* in the heat of the moment at home.

The fifth step is to confide in someone who understands you and believes you. Sometimes, they *already* know that you're being unfairly targeted, or that there isn't any solution to your problem from their end or that the *mm* is in a powerful place, but talking to someone always helps. This support network doesn't solve the problem, but it cushions you emotionally. Sometimes, just knowing someone else sees the truth of your situation can lighten your burden. If patience and time don't seem to bring change, and you feel your spirit sagging, it might be time to move to step number six.

In the sixth step, you establish a buffer to minimize your contact with the *mm*. It can be as simple as limiting interaction with the *mm* or training your mind to think that they do not exist when in reality they are in the next room. Consider arranging any necessary interactions to be short and in settings that allow for a quick and graceful exit. Sometimes, such distancing tactics can offer temporary relief, but if your peace of mind remains under siege, it's time to consider more definitive boundaries.

Reducing the frequency and depth of your interactions can serve as a crucial safeguard to your mental health, ensuring you engage on your terms, briefly and less frequently, without compromising your well-being.

The seventh step is about asserting yourself and setting definitive boundaries. This is the point where you decide that enough is enough and it's time to take more drastic measures for the sake of your own well-being. For instance, consider Mariam, who endured her father-in-law's demanding quirks because her husband would make up for it with thoughtful gifts and cash, and her mother-in-law treated her exceptionally well, even securing a plot of land in her name. On the other hand, Batool faced a different scenario. Her youngest sister-in-law's constant undermining pushed her to the brink of anxiety. Unlike Mariam, Batool couldn't find a silver lining, leading her to call for a crucial family meeting. While this bold move stirred up immediate discomfort and led to accusations flying, it was a necessary step towards establishing her place and asserting her needs within the family. This drastic step, though fraught with tension, ultimately paved the way for a more respectful and considerate relationship. It's a clear message: this step should be the last resort, employed only when all other methods have failed and the cost to your mental health becomes too great to bear without action. This step, though fraught with risks, can unfold in various ways—some may lead to resolution, while others might exacerbate the issues. The examples of the latter happening are too saddening to state, so we will only stick with hopeful stories; the times when taking a stand brings about a positive change, even if it's gradual. Remember, *mms* are *mms* for a reason. They often earn this title because of their enduring, challenging nature; altering their behavior can seem a Herculean task, and removing them from your life is seldom an option. They are a persistent part of your world, woven into the fabric of your daily interactions— that marker stain on a bedsheet you can't throw away - till death do us part. Hence, while it's important to manage expectations, maintaining hope is equally crucial as it fuels the courage needed to assert your boundaries and advocate for your peace.

Handling life with an *mm - a massi musibatein*, is less about enduring hardship and more about safeguarding your own joy—it's about self-care on a heroic scale. Consider Zuni, a dear friend who prefers BFC over KFC and will give you two hundred reasons why, who has mastered this art beautifully. Every evening, she returns to a house where peace is scarce, thanks to her two *nands* who can't seem to stop stirring the pot. Yet, they adore her sons, and moving out isn't financially feasible. So, Zuni carves out sanctuaries of serenity through her hobbies, crafting moments of tranquility amid the turmoil.

It's a delicate balance, keeping your spirit buoyant in choppy waters. While we might not change the difficult characters in our lives, we can certainly adjust our sails. For Zuni, and for anyone in her small flats, it's about finding what refuels your soul and embracing it. And when the waves of drama threaten to pull you under, sometimes the best rescue is as simple as *hanging up the phone*. In the grand theater of family dramas, preserving your peace is the strongest act of self-care.

——

Dear Ayesha,

Long before the 1947 partition, when Lahore was still known as Loh-Kot, Mian Mehmood Shahnawaz's second wife, who was Hindu, gave birth to a son named Zulifkar Mehmood. Over time, Zulifkar realized that his father despised him, believing he had given his father reasons to do so; his slow speech, his inability to learn his father's craft, and his dull, sand-like complexion. But when Zulifkar married Zubaida Parveen, he couldn't fathom why his father also despised his wife, as she had proven to be a brilliant woman and an even more exceptional daughter-in-law than any of his brothers' wives. There was no reason, not a single one, for his father to hate his wife, yet he still did. As the sun set and the moon rose, Zulifkar vowed never to be like his father.

However, when Zulifkar's son, Phool, learned to walk late, to talk late, to talk back, and to walk ahead, Zulifkar began to despise him. He thought he couldn't be a good father to a 'bad' son who was giving him reasons to think so. Then, when Phool married a tribal woman, Zulifkar despised her too, simply for existing. He had become what he once hated.

Loh-Kot has since become Lahore, but the same story repeats in nearly every other house. Some families carry generational trauma that perpetuates and normalizes behaviors that should never be normalized. If you cannot break it, then you should not bear it. Life is too short to grieve and pass on grief, but becomes too long once that grief has passed.

Love, the jinns.

Chapter 10

Happily Ever After

The following points are extremely important and knowledgeable pieces of advice. Do what you may with them for they hold immense power to completely alter your marriage.

Bakery A has a cake that looks delicious. It is advertised to be delicious. Everyone wants it. When they put it up for sale, you go get it. It does not taste good. It gives you a stomachache. The chocolate stings your teeth and you don't even have weak teeth. But you keep quiet because Bakery A is known, it is what everyone wants and you've landed their cake. Plus, they wrapped the cake up in a red collectible ribbon (that is of no use). Bakery B is down the street, and it's not always crowded like Bakery A, but their cake is light and spongy and the aftertaste is like summer season in your mouth. The packaging isn't the best and you have to refrigerate it to consume it but that cake *suits* you. You can have it daily with *chai*. Choose Bakery B. This advice isn't about choosing a good cake.

If you have dressed a certain way all your life and done things that are drastically different from your husband-to-be, and you're constantly worrying about the discomfort you're going to face, but you're told that this discomfort is nothing compared to the generational wealth you're gaining, don't listen. Unlearning twenty-five years of your life and going against your comfort is not compromising; it's letting go of a part of yourself for no valid reason other than *this is just how things are here.*

A vessel needs to be emptied for a new drink to be poured into it. Clear your heart of *the one who got away* before you settle for a new man.

Hand over the chocolates yourself, but don't allow the snack drawer to be opened in your absence. Yes, it's only chocolate today. Tomorrow, it won't be. Set boundaries from day one.

No matter how many servants are in the big mansion you're moving into, if the *saas* was expected to cook all her life, you will likely have to cook as well. So, either learn how to cook or marry into a desi family where a *saas* does not cook.

The *dewar* is not your responsibility, and never will be.

If there are children in the house and you're bringing something home, don't forget to bring something for the children, *especially* if they're not yours.

Your mother-in-law will never be your *ama jee* and you will never be her *beti.* You're her *bahu* and she's your *saas*, and maintaining respect and consideration and a lot of hesitance will keep the relationship crack-free.

If you did not grasp the point above: No matter how much you make her *like your mother,* if you're in a drowning boat, she will still save her stubborn elder daughter who forgets to fetch her water. You can't replace blood relations.

Always be happy if a son spends on his mother.

Your husband should not come home to your sad face six days in a row. Don't ever let him regret coming home.

Learn to give your man love before you give him a tough time, even if it's a love marriage. He must experience the good moments before the bad ones.

Never trust the house servant.

The gold is yours. Unless your man can wear the chain and showcase the bling-bling ring, it's not his to keep.

If you're mature enough to have sex, you're mature enough to take care of your gold, from both sides. It does not need to be kept in some unknown factory in the name of safety.

Love your man a little extra if he pays the *zakat* amount on your gold. But, if he doesn't, you need to take care of it yourself. Never neglect to pay *zakat.*

It's never okay for other house member(s) to sleep in your room unless their room is being painted, the wall has fallen, or more than six lizards are haunting it. But even then, it should only be a once-in-a-lifetime occurrence.

If his little siblings love ice cream, bring it for them on your way home. Don't make a face when they invite themselves to go with you because you couldn't stop yourself from tagging them along the first hundred times.

Your husband should give you pocket money. It's a no-brainer. And then he should forget that he gave it.

Dates are very important. In fact, they are so important that you might need to take a day off from anything and everything to go on one. Even if you are in the middle of a nerve-wracking fight, get ready, smell good, and drive off to a nice place. Everything else can wait.

Guests and family sit on the sofas, and if there are no sofas, they sit outside the room. Your bed is never an option. No one but you and your husband should sit on your bed. Some people feel very strongly about this, and if you're not one of those people, life will be a little easier for you.

Eat in silence if you are with the whole family.

Cranberry juice sachets from the local pharmacy are the solution for a summertime, post-marriage UTI.

Remember, the walls might not have ears, but the six people living in the house do. And sometimes they love to eavesdrop.

Privacy is precious. Keep certain things between just the two of you. If your husband shares your secrets or anything that you've said outside the room with anyone, he's not a good husband. And if you do that, you need to stop. (Unless it's something not normal. Telling your wife that you dream about your male best friend with excitement is not normal.)

You won't agree on everything, but it is important to be fair and respectful during disagreements. If the matter is heating up, talk to him after some time.

Don't keep bringing up the past. Everyone makes mistakes. Learn to forgive and move on. Cheating is not a mistake. Neither is any sort of abuse.

If he spits the food out and leaves the table because the *aloo salan* has too much salt, he might leave the marriage. You can too.

If you don't find that joke to be funny, then it is not a joke.

That not funny joke in front of relatives that keeps you up at night does not mean that you're overly sensitive.

If he can mistreat his mother, he *will* mistreat you.

A woman should never have to forcefully earn. If you're happy in the means that the husband has, you shouldn't have to step foot out of the house.

Give compliments freely to your in-laws.

You are his number one priority, and if you have children, you both are his top priority. No buts. And if you're left asking for more when the brother and sister-in-law or others perfectly capable of earning are enjoying your husband's savings, it is never going to be a happy marriage.

I don't know who needs to hear this but no matter how bad the inflation in the country gets, no woman should have to split the bill for the air conditioner just because she sits under it too.

There is never just one slap. Learn from the movies.

If he repeatedly avoids intimacy in the marriage, something is definitely wrong.

Do not make a good man beg for sex.

Fighting is inevitable but broadcasting it outside the bedroom can be controlled.

If he can sleep peacefully while you cry, it may be that he's extremely tired, or that he just does not care. Usually, it's the latter.

Don't give your opinion to the in-laws unless they ask for it.

If you act like a doormat, never knowing when to stop, you'll be more used than the mat bought on sale from Al-Fatah right outside the main door.

Do not eat before the deed no matter how hungry you are.

Sensitive men make great lovers.

Your best friends should never know your husband's weaknesses or about last night's fight. You will make up with your husband, but they will not forget it. You'll either spend all future lunches in Gulberg trying to explain that your husband is in fact a good man, or you'll go home and not like your husband the same.

You deserve orgasms. Orgasms make life so much better. Don't fake them.

Don't smell like instant noodles when your husband comes home.

Your husband is your built-in BFF, but refrain from telling him the secrets of your *maika*.

Female friendships aren't problematic until they are; if you don't like her, he should definitely not be talking to her.

Love might lessen, respect should never.

A mutton lover will not settle for *bhindi*, no matter how deliciously you cook it. It's okay to not like mutton but it's not okay to deprive someone of it knowing that they love it. This advice works in all walks of life.

Trust can be rebuilt but it takes time. It also takes a lot of understanding, remembering the tiniest details, and gifts.

If you cannot communicate with him, you have a serious problem. Whatever the emotion or situation, you should be able to communicate with him at any given time.

A wise person once said that if the relationship is important, forget the problem and if the problem cannot be forgotten, forget the relationship.

The silent treatment is never an option.

Your child should be raised according to your rules and your partner should set the tone straight if you live in a joint family system.

Have your own hobbies that give you joy. You must be happy on your own to be happier with your husband.

Absence makes the heart grow fonder. Sometimes a day or so apart can fix a lot of things.

When you can hear each other clearly, don't shout.

Listen to respond, not to react. The day you learn this difference, you will avoid a lot of conflicts.

He is the best today, but he might not be the same tomorrow if you keep taking him for granted.

It's okay to be the first to apologize sometimes—it shows strength, not weakness. Holding onto your pride after an argument can turn a molehill into a mountain.

Don't try to be his mother. He already has one.

Nothing, absolutely nothing permits you to use the D or T word during a fight in an otherwise happy marriage.

I firmly believe that it is Allah who changes hearts, safeguards the goodness in them, and pours in the unconditional love that your husband has for you. Pray to Him when the love lessens.

Talk to Him in sadness and happiness. He will say *KUN*, and it will happen. Be a little child and request what you want. God is great.

The world is enough to make him feel less of a man but you shouldn't ever do that.

Learn from the past years. Your in-laws might react differently but their thoughts and opinions will not change.

Living together with the in-laws can be both a blessing and a curse.

At one point, you will know your husband more than anyone else in the house so always go with your gut feeling when making decisions that will impact him.

Men do not like to be disturbed in the washroom. Do not knock frantically. His feces have a limit. It will end.

Sharing is not the same as caring when it comes to a toothbrush. There are other ways to be romantic; sharing a toothbrush is not one of them.

You get to name the child no matter how much emotional damage is being done by that one *khala*, *phupho*, or *saas* unless they'll be paying the tuition fees.

If you're safekeeping a family member's possession, write the location down.

If someone in his family thinks you're an awful person or that you purposely put garlic instead of ginger that one time, *let them believe so.* Nothing you do - absolutely no explanation you give will make them believe otherwise. Some people are wired this way. They're not worth any explanation.

Male friendships are healthy, but staying out five times a week until three in the morning is not acceptable.

If the rice, the salad, and the *salan* are nice, someone on the table should have basic manners to compliment the food you made, even if it's a daily occurrence.

Never underestimate the power of a good cup of tea. Sometimes, the best conversations happen over a steaming cup of *chai*, especially if there's a little biscuit on the side to dunk. It's about warmth, both in the cup and in your company.

Every Eid should be spent together, and no matter what the amount, Eidi is a must.

Always know which of his suits are at the dry cleaner's.

The sunlight has a smell and it's very noticeable on *chiffon dupattas.*

Invest in good pillows. Change them after a few years.

The dad bod is only cute until the deed becomes difficult.

Always keep the flame of appreciation burning. Even a simple 'thank you' for the everyday tasks can make your spouse feel valued.

Remember that the perfect partner does not exist. Embrace each other's flaws as much as you celebrate strengths.

Keep the in-laws involved, but set clear boundaries. They are an important part of your life, but they shouldn't dictate how you live it.

Learn not to scream at the sight of a lizard or a spider. Huge in-laws' families usually have *dados* or *dadas* with pacemakers and heart problems.

Sometimes the younger *bahus* have it better.

Silence with a partner you've known for years shouldn't scare you. It is only with people that you don't know well that you have a lot to talk about.

Communicate openly about your finances. Money issues can create significant stress in marriages.

It is difficult to love life as a spice loving individual in a family of blood pressure patients. No amount of bribery will get you the *daal* you want.

Keep the pantry stocked with his favorite snacks.

A kind but "useless-in-the-house-chores-department" *bahu* is always better than a rude one who can make ten rotis in five minutes.

Don't overshare with your *dewranis* and *jethanis,* even if you share the same set of problems.

What life is today is not what life will be five to ten years from now. Have patience.

Celebrate small victories together. Whether it's as minor as fixing a leaky tap in the guest bathroom or as major as getting a promotion.

I love cats but understand that pets are not the same as having human children. Don't try to convince your husband's family otherwise.

Regularly revisit and renegotiate your roles within the marriage as needed. Life changes, and so might your responsibilities towards each other. What worked during the early years of your marriage may need adjustment as you grow older.

Respect personal space as much as shared space. Just because you share a life doesn't mean you can't have your own corners of solitude. Whether it's a reading nook or a spot in the garden, having a little nook where you can be alone is as vital as having a place to come together.

A little humor goes a long way in any marriage. Even during a quarrel, a well-timed joke can turn a frown upside down. Remember, it's not just about making up after fights; it's about not letting the fights get too serious in the first place.

An internet *nano* once said, be like salt; he should not be able to live without you and yet he shouldn't be able to consume you entirely.

If person A tells you about person B, keep what has been told to yourself. Always keep everything to yourself. Be a well. People trust and love wells.

My *nano* once said, *"khud ki choro mat, kisi ko chero mat."* This means that you shouldn't go against what you believe but that doesn't mean that if your in-laws believe in something else, you start to invalidate their opinion.

Unless you marry a man who loves you more than you love him, you will never comprehend the extent to which men can be generous.

Divorce is the last resort, but it's better than growing old with the wrong person.

Don't burden yourself with a person who no longer loves you.

Never make a decision in haste. Take your time to weigh the pros and cons. Breathe in, breathe out. Only when you're in a calm state, free from extreme emotions like anger or excitement, should you make your decision. This approach ensures thoughtful choices that you won't regret later.

If it's not a marriage problem, it's a career issue. If your career is smooth, it'll be a health concern. If your health is perfect, it'll be a child-related challenge. There will always be something despite the time. Learn to find happiness in the midst of chaos. The bedsheet will never be wrinkle-free.

As we wrap up this rollercoaster ride through the kaleidoscope of *desi* marriages, it's been a journey of laughter, tears, spicy gossip, and some good old family drama. Each chapter, each story we've delved into, wasn't just to pass the time—it was to light the way through the sometimes murky waters of matrimonial life in our vibrant culture.

Remember, managing a marriage isn't about charting a flawless course but about enjoying the ride, potholes and all. It's about learning to laugh when the only two samosas that are left burn, to hold hands even when it feels like the end of the world, and to dance in the bedroom when the lounge buzzes with the familiar drama.

And when the going gets tough—when the in-laws test your patience or the *chai* spills over the stove—remember that every great story needs a bit of conflict to make the resolution sweeter. Don't shy away from writing your own witty dialogues and heartfelt monologues.

So, as you flip the last page of this guide, let's not just aim to survive our marriages but to thrive in them, creating stories that aren't just told but celebrated. Go forth with a smile, a plan, and maybe a handy list of tips tucked into your *dupatta*. Remember, every day is a new scene in your family drama—make it count, make it memorable, and above all, make it yours.

In the end, every marriage, every heart, and every home has a story. Make yours a story worth telling.

Chapter 11

Forgetting Faheem

The book has ended. The sun has set. The entertainers have bowed and exited, leaving behind echoes in the empty hall. The curtain falls, signaling the end of the spectacle. But, if your heart hurts, this chapter is your sanctuary.

He met me like he would never leave, and he left as if we had never met.

Love is a black *chaddar*. It envelops you, shrouds your vision, and you see no flaws—just a perfect embrace of undiluted affection. But the true beauty of it is that when you're in love, the worst news in the world feels insignificant. To you, even a smoggy, hazardous, polluted sky is like a breath of fresh air. However, if your love departs, the exact opposite happens; not even the happiest occasions can lift your sinking heart. No joy can buoy the heavy heart that remains, leaving even the sunniest days cloaked in an inescapable gloom.

Walking into marriage, no one plans for its end. Yet, despite the commonness of divorce, there's often a solid belief that your union will endure.

When it was time for the bird to fly, it fell in love with the cage.

It doesn't matter where he's gone - into the arms of another woman, to a place far from you, or to Allah. If he's gone, *he's gone*. No words penned by me, nor shared by those who've traversed this path before, can blunt the raw edge of grief. The grief will unfold with time, the wound will slowly heal, but it might get infected in the process, which is to say that flashbacks in the rearview mirror may choke you, and absolutely nothing in the world can fasten the process. But, it will get better. It always does.

Managing the aftermath of losing him, be it through separation or divorce or even as being strangers in the same house, is like finding your way through a once familiar town now shrouded in fog. Initially, every breath might feel labored, as if you're learning to inhale and exhale all over again under the weight of his *yaad*.

Grief will visit like an uninvited guest at a wedding, lingering long after the function has ended. Some days, it will sit quietly in the corner - letting you know that it's there and on others, it will dance wildly, pulling you into its embrace - whipping the sadness out. Yet, amid this dance, when your legs hurt and your thoughts go numb, there will be moments when something will make you unintentionally smile to remind you that joy isn't permanently erased from your life.

You may want to be left alone but that's not the best for your soul. You're like a child lost in Joyland so treat yourself like one. You need to seek solace in the company of those who can share your silence as comfortably as your stories. Whether it's the wise words of a *nano* who terribly wanted it to work but understands that whatever happens, happens for the best or the empathetic ear of a married sister - allow their support to be the soothing balm. Some *babas* might go quiet. But it is not because he is not with you, it is only because seeing you in pain, pains him. And if the burden weighs too heavily, let a therapist guide you through the tangled emotions with the gentle precision of a tailor untangling threads.

Hold onto hope with the stubbornness of a monsoon cloud refusing to part with its rain. You can get through it. Time, that ancient healer, will gradually ease the pain. Slowly, the world will regain its colours, laughter will find its way back to your lips, and you'll realize that moving forward is not a betrayal of your past but a homage to the resilience of your spirit.

There's an undeniable transformation that comes from loving and leaving. You may find yourself searching for who you were before the marriage ended. Remember, there's solace in the duck theory—embrace the act until you become it. If you act like a duck, walk and talk like a duck, you *eventually become a duck*. Pretending really helps. You might not immediately relish the mango ice cream you once adored, and it might take days before it tastes sweet again, but eventually, you'll find delight in its flavor, scooping joy where you once found none.

As you sift through memories of what was, it's vital to celebrate what now can be. Revel in the liberation of singlehood. There's a certain magic in having the entire bed to yourself, not having to hear the taunts of your *saas*, not being on your toes to always be there for Faheem, choosing late-night movie marathons without a care, and cooking up a storm of your favorite dishes whenever the whim strikes, without being told off about the salt.

Stick to a daily routine. The upheaval of a separation disrupts everything, making the world feel uncertain and unstable. Finding solace in a regular routine can help bring back a sense of normalcy and control, anchoring you during turbulent times. It might feel like the most difficult thing to achieve, but if your routine is stable, your heart *will* find stability too. *Ap chalna shuru ho jaein, dil bhi ahista ahista raah per aa jae ga.*

Forgiveness is crucial. Whether the decision was mutual or one-sided, pain and blame can linger. It's important to forgive—both the other person and yourself. This isn't just about moving on; it's about freeing yourself from the chains of past hurts. Not forgiving means remembering and remembering means hurting. Letting go helps heal your heart. It hurts to see women with kind hearts become vengeful and lose themselves in the process. His betrayal should not be the reason for you becoming a difficult person. *Kuch bhi hou jae,* kuch nahin hota. *Wou ap kay begair nahin murra, ap bhi baar baar, har din, us ko yaad kar kay na murein.*

Aunties will talk, the *ghar wale* will talk the most—it's as inevitable as the monsoon rains soaking through the bustling markets. Each whisper, each sidelong glance at a family gathering, might seem like the beat of a *dhol* that calls attention not to celebration but to scrutiny. Yet, let this not dismay you.

How you handle this chatter matters. With grace and poise, you can turn each whisper into a breeze that passes by unnoticed. Remember, the murmurs of others are mere echoes; they do not define the solid ground on which you stand. Respond with a gentle smile, a clever deflection—turn their curiosity into admiration for your resilience. You know your truth and your journey—no one else has walked in your shoes. *Jou kehte hain kehne dou. Loug hain, unka kaam hai kehna.*

The child may have his egoistic behavior, his *badaam-*coloured eyes, and his habit of playfully burping after a good meal. Even when he grows out of his father's habits, he will look more and more like his father than he ever did and *it is alright.* Do not take your frustration out on the most beautiful thing that came out of a failed marriage.

There will be times when you will dream of him, and it will frighten you out of sleep for days in a row, knowing that if you meet him again in a dream, your heart will long to meet him when you're awake. But know this: to him, you might not even be a thought, let alone a long night's dream. In those moments of vulnerability, remind yourself of your worth. His absence does not diminish your value, nor does it define your future. Remember, you are stronger than you know, braver than you feel, and more loved than you realize.

For those long nights when everyone has slept, but the world feels too vast and your heart too heavy, turn to Allah. Imagine every prayer as a heartfelt dialogue, where you lay down the weights of your soul. He doesn't just listen; He responds. In the depth of *sujood*, when your forehead touches the prayer mat in utter surrender, feel the closeness—how tenderly He understands your unspoken words, your deepest fears, and your silent tears. This relationship with Allah, it's more meaningful than any earthly bond. He loves you more intensely than anyone ever could—seventy times more than your own mother. This connection, this divine companionship, is the truest comfort, the deepest peace you can find. *Aye, ibne Adam. Ek teri chahat hai aur ek meri chahat hai, hoga wohi jo meri chahat hai. Haan agar tune supurd kar diya khud ko uske jo meri chahat hai, tou main tujhe baksh doonga wou bhi jo teri chahat hai. Aur agar tune nafarmani ki uski jo meri chahat hai, tou main thaka dunga tujhe us mein jo teri chahat hai. Phir hoga wohi jo meri chahat hai.*

Take it one day at a time. Thinking about all that lies ahead can be overwhelming. Instead, focus on getting through each day with *sabr* and *shukar*. Each morning brings a new start, and each night is a step closer to healing.

Young Malik Muzaffar Saeed

My dear baba, the man every man should be. To love endlessly is to be him. To give from empty cupboards is to be him. To think of you when no one thinks of him is to be him. To forget the roads his feet are most familiar with because your destination is different is to be him. To offer a smile when the world offers none is to be him. To be the sweetest Multani mango on the tip of a virgin tongue is to be him. To breathe life into forgotten corners of old, worn-out rooms of Model Town houses where no beings live, is to be him. To exist in silences that hold stories is to be him. To live and love and live a life that can be loved is to be him.